MW01438925

*Off the Map:*
*Vancouver Writers With Lived Experience of*
*Mental Health Issues*

Edited by
Betsy Warland
Seema Shah
Kate Bird

# Off the Map

Vancouver writers with
lived experience of
mental health issues

bell press
anthologies

bellpressbooks.com
Bluesky: @bellpressbooks.bsky.social
Instagram: @bellpressbooks

OFF THE MAP


ISBN 978-1-7387167-8-4 (print) | ISBN 978-1-7387167-9-1 (ebook)

Edited by Betsy Warland, Seema Shah, and Kate Bird
Cover art: *Please Explain* by Seema Shah, previously published in *Contemporary Collage Magazine*, Issue #21
Copyediting by Devon Field

LIBRARY AND ARCHIVES CANADA CATALOGUING IN PUBLICATION

Title: Off the map : Vancouver writers with lived experience of mental health issues.
Other titles: Off the map (Vancouver, B.C.)
Identifiers: Canadiana (print) 20250160331 | Canadiana (ebook) 2025016230X | ISBN 9781738716784 (softcover) | ISBN 9781738716791 (EPUB)
Subjects: LCSH: Mentally ill, Writings of the, Canadian—British Columbia—Vancouver. | LCSH: Recovering addicts' writings. | LCSH: Recovering alcoholics' writings. | LCSH: Canadian literature—21st century. | LCSH: Canadian literature—British Columbia—Vancouver. | CSH: Mentally ill, Writings of the, Canadian (English)—British Columbia—Vancouver. | CSH: Recovering addicts' writings, Canadian (English)—British Columbia—Vancouver. | CSH: Recovering alcoholics' writings, Canadian (English)—British Columbia—Vancouver. | CSH: Canadian literature (English)—21st century | CSH: Canadian literature (English)—British Columbia—Vancouver. | LCGFT: Poetry. | LCGFT: Creative nonfiction. | LCGFT: Fiction.
Classification: LCC PS8235.M45 O33 2025 | DDC C810.8/0920740971133—dc23

Bell Press publishes and operates on the unceded Coast Salish Territories of the xʷməθkʷəy̓əm (Musqueam), Sḵwx̱wú7mesh (Squamish), and səl̓ilwətaʔɬ (Tsleil-Waututh) Nations.

"An extremely vital and intimate collection on living with mental illness, offering an abundance of insight and hope to readers. The writers of this anthology gift us their vulnerable and brave selves with astonishing honesty as they mime some of their darkest, most discomfiting moments of their lives for clarity. *Off the Map* is an orchestra of richness and compassion."

—Lindsay Wong, author of *The Woo-Woo* and *Tell Me Pleasant Things about Immortality*

"Whatever heals or helps, it's often not a straight-forward process and the 33 talented writers in *Off the Map* document the multifarious twists and turns to living, healing and destigmitizing mental health matters. Humour abounds in this multi-genre collection that packs surprise and insights within the circuitous strategies of literary craft."

—Kevin Spenst, author of *A Bouquet Brought Back from Space*

# Contents

## Foreword



## Creative Nonfiction

## Fiction



## Poetry

CONTENT NOTE: Some pieces in this anthology explore topics related to mental health and may be distressing to some individuals.

# Foreword

## Betsy Warland

In my experience as an author, teacher, and mentor, we writers cling to the assumption that the act of writing will get easier over the years. In reality, it grows more challenging. Every piece we write—whether it is a poem or a novel—is counting on us to faithfully evoke it regardless of genre, subject matter, and what we have successfully written in the past. Our job is to put our ear to each specific narrative ground and carefully listen, to trust it knows where it is going and what it is about. Humbling? Yes. But fascinating. I've come to believe that the act of writing faithfully is my greatest teacher.

The revered and quirky American poet Emily Dickinson knew this. She wrote: "Tell all the truth but tell it slant." The *Off the Map* writers also offer a compelling honesty, inventiveness, and compassion. They are writers with lived experience of mental health issues. A refreshing quality we editors appreciated in the *OTM* writers' work is their directness, hard-won insight, and originality.

The poetry, creative nonfiction, and fiction in this anthology cover a wide range of subject matter. Some writers wrote deeply personal stories about their own mental health and/or substance use struggles, while others wrote about a variety of other experiences including street life, family, immigration, identity, a beloved cat, learning to drum, and even futuristic technology. This collection aims to both highlight the creativity and diversity of writing by individuals with lived experience of mental health issues, and introduce new talent to the literary community.

Much new talent came to our attention through Professional Artistic Growth Made Accessible (PAGMA), a project that offers free professional development opportunities for Vancouver writers and artists with lived experience of mental health and/or substance use issues. In 2022, writer and artist Seema Shah (who I met several years ago via an anthology) invited me to join the project. She has received funding for the project from Vancouver Coastal Health's Consumer Initiative Fund (CIF), an innovative program that funds community projects proposed by residents of Vancouver, British Columbia, with lived experience of these issues.

In 2023 and 2024, as PAGMA's writing expert, I provided one-on-one writing consults and delivered skills-oriented workshops. Impressed with the writers' work, and recognizing that many participants had not yet been published, Seema and I began exploring the idea of an anthology. We were thrilled that Bell Press, a relatively new Vancouver publisher that specializes in anthologies, accepted our proposal for *Off the Map* and that CIF approved a grant to help support the editing process. Suddenly we were in a tailwind.

Needing to expand our team, we invited Kate Bird to be a co-editor. Kate was not only a workshop participant, but is an extensively published author who I knew through The Writer's Studio at SFU. Kate's skills have been invaluable. The three of us co-facilitated writing workshops, in which we offered feedback on pieces that participants planned to submit to *Off the Map*. We also worked one-on-one with contributors after acceptance to further revise their work for publication.

Due to CIF criteria, our call for submissions was limited to residents of the City of Vancouver, located on the unceded lands of the xʷməθkʷəy̓əm (Musqueam), Sḵwx̱wú7mesh (Squamish), and səlilwətaɬ (Tsleil-Waututh) Nations.

Several writers in surrounding areas wanted to submit, but we had to decline. We made a concerted effort to reach out to local mental health programs, as well as university writing programs and literary associations. We anticipated maybe 30 submissions.

We were stunned—we received 63 submissions.

We were also delighted by the quality of the writing. The writing was very strong and the range of subject matter compelling. Given space limitations, we had to make tough decisions, taking into consideration content, genres, styles, and subject matter. We also wanted to include BIPOC writers, 2SLGBTQIA+ writers, and writers with disabilities, and represent writers from different age groups, ethnicities, and social backgrounds.

Several contributors have long-standing connections to important community mental health arts groups and organizations. And, in keeping with the anthology's concept, we prioritized unpublished and emerging writers over more established ones. Fourteen of the anthology's 33 contributors were workshop participants.

Along the way, we searched for other anthologies featuring writers with lived experience of mental health issues. *Hidden Lives: True Stories from People who Live with Mental Illness* (Lenore Rowntree & Andrew Boden, eds., Brindle & Glass 2012, 2nd edition 2017) features first-hand accounts by people living with mental illness and their family members. *Inside the Bell Jar* literary journal and *Workman Arts*, a multidisciplinary mental health organization, have also produced anthologies in Canada. Simply stated: more anthologies like this are in order.

We believe *Off the Map* is a unique and important addition to the literary landscape, one we hope will challenge readers' preconceived ideas about writers with lived experience of mental health issues, as well as their writing. Even after going through the process of revisions and our increasing familiarity with each author's writing, we still are moved and delighted by their work.

If you long for depth, originality, poignant honesty, surprise, and delight, you will find it here, in *Off the Map*. Between these covers.

# Waiting for the Greenhouse Effect

Seema Shah

Plants don't do well under my care. I wish I knew why because I'd love to have an apartment full of flowers and greenery.

My fondness for foliage goes back to childhood—this is evident in my very first poem, which I penned at the age of eight:

*Nature is beautiful*
*Nature is fun*
*Nature is sometimes*
*In the sun*

As an adult, I tried numerous times to adorn my apartment with plant life. I did my best to tend to these plants and give them a good home—water, sunlight, the whole bit. But no matter how hard I tried, it didn't take long before I was surrounded by plant death.

Hoping to avoid this outcome, I bought many a "hardy" plant which I was assured I'd have to "go out of my way to kill."

Even these supposedly robust specimens met an early demise when they moved in with me.

So you'll understand why I had reservations about horticultural therapy while attending an inpatient creative arts therapy program I'll call Meadowside. The program offered a variety of therapies, including art therapy, music therapy, and recreation therapy. Some were mandatory, and some, like horticultural therapy, were optional.

Despite my hesitation, I signed up for horticultural therapy. This was a one-time opportunity, and I wasn't going to let my horticultural history hold me back. From what the Canadian Horticultural Therapy Association's website had to say, it sounded like this therapeutic modality had potential:

*"Gardening and horticulture is intrinsically healing and can be enjoyed at many levels including active involvement in the form of planting and maintaining a garden as well as the passive enjoyment of simply sitting in a garden. Both have been documented to increase happiness, contentment, and overall well-being."*

I did enjoy sitting in gardens. And, as far as I knew, I hadn't killed any plants by doing this.

However, horticultural therapy wasn't what I'd envisioned. It didn't seem much like a horticultural experience, nor was it particularly therapeutic.

So much for sitting in the garden and soaking up the sunshine, as all of our sessions took place indoors in the evening. Sure, we were in a greenhouse, and it was still light out when we started at 6 p.m., but something didn't seem quite right.

*Session #1: Aromatherapy*

I realize aromatherapy uses essential oils derived from plants, but calling it horticultural therapy seemed like a bit of a stretch. And it wasn't like we spent the session learning to make essential oils. The instructor just passed around vials of different oils which we sniffed as he explained their healing properties.

He also showed us a few Meadowside-made products, such as lotions and spritzers, that contained various combinations of essential oils. We didn't make any of these concoctions, although we were given a few "recipes" to make at home. However, we could buy them directly from the Horticulture Department, if we wanted to shell out $20 for a small container.

After learning about these products, we moved on to the next step: giving each other lengthy, step-by-step hand massages using Meadowside Hand Cream. Don't ask me. As we sat across the narrow table from each other, hand in hand, curious passers-by stopped and stared down at us from a large window that overlooked the greenhouse. They were probably as confused as we were. Maybe this exercise was supposed to make us realize how therapeutic hand massages with this special lotion were, so that we'd stock up right away and start on the road to wellness.

*Session #2: Herbal Vinegars*

Although we used herbs in our second session, it seemed more like a cooking class than anything else. The entire session was dedicated to making our very own bottle of herbal vinegar. The measured-out herbs had already been laid out in an organized fashion on a paper place mat in front of each vinegar-maker. We were given a tall bottle, into which we placed each herb in the order given by the instructor. After this, we poured in the star ingredient and sealed the bottle shut. I did not find this very therapeutic.

We then had two options: either spend $15 and buy the vinegar we just made or leave it behind to be sold. At this point, I sensed a pattern emanating from Meadowside's "green" house.

*Session #3: Botanical Prints*

We used flower petals in our third session, but making botanical prints seemed more like an art class than anything else.

I found this activity about as therapeutic as making a bottle of herbal vinegar.

Identical settings of petals from various plants had already been placed in front of each botanical print-maker, along with a white sheet of paper. We were told exactly where to place each petal on the sheet… a petals-by-numbers of sorts. When all of our petals had been glued down in just the right spot and our picture was complete, we chose one of the many coloured and shaped mattes available to us for mounting.

We then had two options: either spend $10 and buy the botanical print we just made or leave it behind to be sold at what I now call the "Horticulture Gift Shop."

*Session #4: Herbal Butters and Jams*

I assumed we would be making herbal butters and jams in our final session, not *eating* them. I was wrong. This session was more like dinner than anything else.

We spread a variety of already-made herbal butters on different types of bread and a variety of already-made herbal jams on homemade scones, and we sipped a couple of already-made herbal teas. Though I did enjoy these delicacies, I question whether consuming them can really be considered horticultural therapy.

As with the aromatherapy and herbal vinegar sessions, we were sent home with recipes for the butters and jams. It's been months since I left Meadowside and I have yet to make any of these items. Chronic depression doesn't lend itself well to gourmet cooking.

Meadowside's "Return to Function" course, designed to help with the transition back home, even emphasized the fact that basic meal preparation is a daunting task when one is severely depressed. A distinction was made between "light-energy," "medium-energy," and "high-energy" meals.

For example, a granola bar would be considered a "low-energy" breakfast, while cereal would be considered a "medium-energy" breakfast. You actually need to have cereal, milk, a clean bowl, and a clean spoon to have a bowl of cereal, not to mention the dirty dishes you are left with. We weren't given examples of "high-energy" meals, but I'm guessing our herbal concoctions would be above and beyond the high end of our energy scale.

I can't say I was sad when it was time for me to say goodbye to Horticultural Therapy. I still call it that, even though I think it's a misnomer for what I experienced at Meadowside. Something like *A Hint of Horticultural* or *How to Profit from Plant Life* would be more accurate. You'll notice I've left the "Therapy" part out completely. Although others may have found some therapeutic value in these sessions, I failed to experience any personal (or plant) growth in the greenhouse.

# Some techniques for telling your story—when you don't want to talk about your story

Tove Black

Maybe this is common for writers who have PTSD.

I have this story that I really don't want to tell, and yet whatever I write—creative nonfiction, lyrics, or fiction—this is the story that is always trying to insert itself.

So why don't I just tell it? Sometimes I wonder too, but that uncertainty never lasts long before I remember the reasons:

- No one will believe me
- No one wants to read it
- It will make even more people angry at me
- It fucks me up too much to think about it, even after all the therapy—and I still need to be able to do ordinary things like get out of bed and go to work, so I can't afford to get that fucked up.

In other words, I feel a constant push-pull between a story that insists on being told and my horror of telling it.

*

When I think about how I navigate this tension in my writing, I can see a few patterns. Maybe I can even call them techniques.

Maybe I can even give them names:

**1. The donut**

Circle around the things you can't say. (This can also look more like a spiral, but the key is the hollow centre.)

**2. The star**

The reverse of the donut: establish a safe centre and stay there for most of the story, only occasionally and very briefly referring to something outside of it. (Some of these references go further than others.)

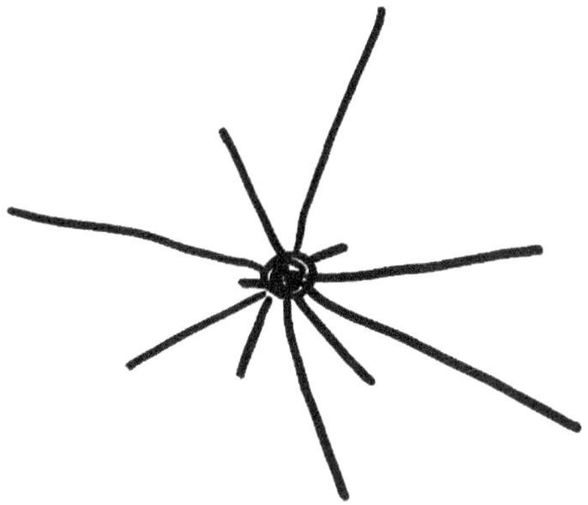

**3. Parallel lines**

Stick as close to the things that actually happened as you have the courage to, but never quite state them.

**4. Avant garde**

Be a cubist or an abstract painter or create a John Cage composition with words—capture the essence without revealing the things you cannot say, adapting techniques from other art forms (including but not limited to abstraction, flashes of imagery, irregular rhythms, mashups, silence).

**5. Just whatever**

Mix up the fiction and nonfiction, be the unreliable narrator, be your own boss.

(Optional but honestly pretty attractive: stick it to the man; fuck the narrative arc. The important thing is to do whatever is necessary to avoid what you need to avoid.)

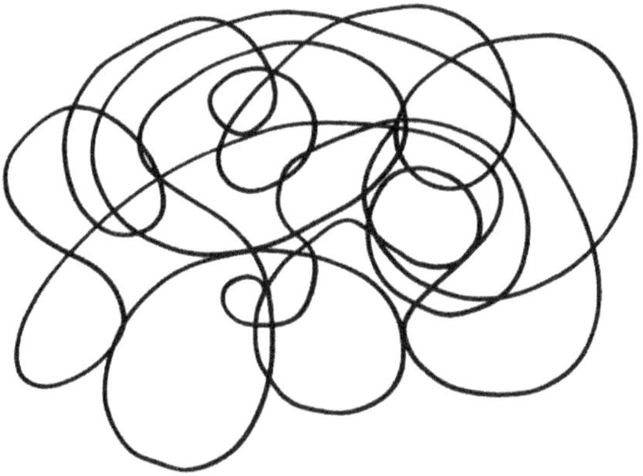

*

Are there rules for these techniques?

No.

And if there were, you would need to break them.

# True Blue

Sandra Yuen

Floating on the true blue of the sea
Not an ordinary blue
But an iridescent aqua
The kind you buy in the acrylic aisle
It cost more than a nickel
But I don't give a hoot

I'm painting a chair
A fresh coat to stop me
from climbing the walls

Welcoming warmth
Sturdy carved calves from old forests
Back that doesn't break

I want to sit on a cloud
And watch the geese fly by
Listening to radio shows
Sipping on sugar pop

I will sit on that chair
Until the wee hours
Dreaming of midnight strolls and candles
Never to stir
Except for
The one who left me
Stranded in an ocean of drowned souls

# *Like a pencil*

Sandra Yuen

I am weightless
like a pencil
floating on crests of waves

like an astronaut
without gravity boots
like heaven
like peace
joy
humility
fun times
or laughter
that comes from your gut
bubbles up
tickling your tongue and tonsils

we want
I want
to be weightless
effortless
variable

like the change from rain to sleet
clouds to sunshine
dusk to dawn

I am weightless
diving into the ether
the void
emerging like a violet phoenix
from a black hole

jet ready to soar

# Dramatization of a Love Story Over and Over

Sandra Yuen

**Part I**

Monday: I met a girl
Tuesday: Fell in love
Wednesday: Flew to Vegas
Thursday: Fought like hounds
Friday: Her husband showed up
Saturday: I was in emerg
Sunday: She left me

**Part II**

Sometimes it's better to have loved and lost
Than never loved at all
Your heart breaks
Life melts like snowflakes
The world shrinks to four walls and a bed
No one to talk to

No one to see
Just cold beans and tuna

Can't work
Can't think
Can't breathe

Alone in misery
Until the next thrill
Or hope of another chance

**Part III**

It was until death does us part
Until the war began
Slicing and dicing
Battle over chores
People spouting nonsense

Our iguana disappeared
And you got laid off again
We burned down the garage
Neighbours chagrined

I left in the wee hours
Knapsack on my shoulder
Never to return
Except for my iPod
To listen to sad songs

And scream

# *Turmoil*

Sandra Yuen

Turmoil is when you're on the highway
fifty miles from nowhere
and the car overheats
your phone is dead
you walk for three hours in the dark
find a motel with no vacancy
restaurants are closed
run out of cigarettes
starts to rain
shoes soak through
turns to sleet
you fall in the mud
can't get up
no cops
no ambulance
no one for miles

you see a glow in the distance
it gets closer
a white sedan pulls up

in a tight dress
a perfumed woman alights
smiles and extends her gloved hand
you reach out
instead she pockets your wallet
nods and drives off

that's turmoil

# Shine like the morning sun

Sandra Yuen

Don't despair in your field of wild tanglewood
Don't fret like a guitar without strings
Don't worry and ruminate
Ponder the unanswerable difficult questions
Or jump to wrong conclusions

Instead shine like the morning sun
Glisten like stones in the dappling creek catching the rays
Sparkle like the rings on Liberace's fingers
Or clean silverware after a douse of Palmolive and quick rinse
Glow like the moon
Amber flame of a candle burning all night
Lighting the path to human kindness and forgiveness

Be happy
More than content
Be ecstatic
Laugh and feel the joy bubbles

And lastly
Don’t Panic

# An Exercise in Drumming

Sandra Yuen

There is nothing easy about it. Drumming on a drum kit is harder than it looks. Yes, you can pound away and believe you are a star, but it takes years, if not decades of practice. First you must learn the bass drum using a kick pedal on the one and the three. Then you hit the snare on the two and the four while gently tapping the hihat with a drumstick in your other hand on every eighth.

Then you start changing when you hit the accent. Sometimes on the upbeat or the downbeat or on the 1 e and ah, 2 e and ah. Suddenly there's more beats between and you aren't to hit the snare but the tom or do a double stroke. Or a triple stroke, a ghost note here or there on the snare or the kick drum, then quickly open the hihat after you hit the snare but before you come in on the kick drum on the three.

Sometimes you have to hit everything all at once or play each drum independently like you have four brains or put in a gap and count in your head, praying you'll get it right in front of two hundred listeners. Or you won't get the gig, freeze, get cut, or something worse!

Practise your meter. Practise your sticking. Pivot the drumstick between your thumb and fingers. Paradiddles are endless. And after you attempt to learn perfect time, the band throws you a curve and you need to swing the beat while keeping the groove in time. Memorizing 200 bars in a song which may vary between intro, verse, chorus, and bridge plus the other 50 songs in the repertoire of your genre. Jazz is different from blues is different from country, disco, Motown, punk, rock and roll, industrial, etcetera etcetera.

It becomes an obsession, a money pit of sorts, but the mere mention of drumming and I salivate. Thanks for listening. You drummed it out of me.

# Linus

Venge Dixon

Travelling east. Driving an old, souped-up pickup truck named Amadeus. I hadn't driven for ten years, nor had I driven anything bigger than a sedan. A blind run from defeat, shame. Agony. East. East. And further east. Because east is not west.

Defeat, shame, and agony arrived a week or so after I did. Like "Big Bear" Bob Hite said, "Wherever you go, there you are."

I bought a 100-year-old, falling-down house in Murphy Cove, a small community on the Eastern Shore. I had three neighbours, each a half-acre and more apart, from me and one another. I knew none of them. This complemented my uncertainty. I settled in.

Howling into the beauty of silence. Waiting for the right moment to end my life. Quietly. Far away from family, not wanting to bequeath them the funeral arrangements. I was a brokenness, squatted over by egoism and self-doubt.

*

The work of winter wore me down: splitting, carrying, stacking wood, chopping kindling, shovelling snow, shovelling snow, shovelling snow, crawling around the basement with a hairdryer thawing frozen pipes. I became a skeleton with muscle bumps on my arms and legs. My money seemed to be evaporating. I had little food. I was hungry.

*

A year passed.

*

Linus came to live with me when he was two—or maybe two and a half, maybe three. The story of his age—as relayed to me by others—continually changed. He grew older the closer we came to our first introduction.

He was young, I was tired

He was afraid. I was afraid. And both of us had been abandoned by circumstance.

*

A friend from Halifax called. She said, "There's this cat…"

"No, I—"

She hurried on, "…his human has Alzheimer's, she's a lesbian, like us. She is in hospital. Her partner has been denied visiting rights. Her children say that their lawyer is coming to take the cat to be euthanized."

"No. I can't. I can't take care of anyone, not even myself."

She called again. "He's a beautiful cat. He's on the kill list at the shelter and he's only two years old…he will die in two weeks. The lawyer is coming… the lawyer is coming."

Then, reluctantly, "*Only* if you can't find somebody else. You really must try. I can't take care of a cat. I don't want a cat! I don't need a cat!"

And on it went, his execution date coming closer and closer. My friend's calls more urgent. Then the cat's neighbour called. "His name is Linus. He is amazing! He can leap from the bottom floor to a second story window. His owner was unintentionally cruel, due to her illness, and kept him tethered to her bedpost for fear he'd escape…"

My friend, again. "The lawyer is coming tomorrow."

And in response to my hesitation, "He will keep the mice out of your house!"

I began to say, "I don't have any…" when a mouse ran across the floor in front of me. I sighed.

"Okay. Bring him."

I sat in my leaky old house, in the middle of the coldest Nova Scotia winter in one hundred years. Waiting for the cat I did not want.

*

Some years later I learned that the shelter where Linus was to be sent had a no-kill policy.

*

Linus arrived at night. The wind was a madness of snow and small branches. My friend handed me Linus's carrier—he scrunched ball-like in that cage and stared at me with what I decided to interpret as terror. "Here is his litter box, his litter, his food, his bowl, his hairbrush. I need to go—the storm is here!" She raced for her truck.

Indoors, as I opened the carrier door, Linus uncoiled, a wire-sprung snake exploding from a peanut-brittle tin. I froze, gobsmacked by the length of him, his speed. He was gone, racing. He disappeared into dark rooms, screeching up the wooden stairs and down and up and down again. I sat. Waited for him. Waited for my heart to stop yammering. He was in my lap—he was off and running. A thud came from the kitchen. I reached the door in time to see him leap from the top of the refrigerator with a bag of fresh muffins clenched between his teeth. I put his food and water bowls down. He showed disdain: *Muffins! Muffins! Muffins!*

What I had interpreted as his terror was my own. A cat. Damn it! A cat! What the hell was I thinking agreeing to take him? A crazy, loooong, liquid, muffin-stealing cat. How would I proceed with my plan to kill myself now? I couldn't just leave him here on his own. I couldn't take care of him. I didn't know how. I couldn't take care of my own mad self! Damn it.

How either of us slept that night I don't remember. Perhaps we didn't. My bed at the time was a leaky air mattress. Or maybe it wasn't leaking yet. He had sharp, non-retracting claws. Winter was brutal. Ice formed, hard and a quarter of an inch thick on the inside windowpane. Strangers, we slept together for warmth those early weeks.

*

I'd read that a cat needs at least seven days to adjust to a new environment and must be kept inside for that length of time. Exactly, I concluded. Seven days and no sooner.

On the third day he escaped, shoving past me as I opened the door. So cautiously! Caution be damned, Linus raced for the trees. I raced for my wellies. Outside I began to panic—he was gone! He would be eaten by coyotes, run over on the highway, buried in high snow! Then I heard him crying loudly. Yowling. This sound crashed into my heart like a fatal accident. I stumbled and crawled my way through waist-high snow towards his terrifying wails. I was crying. Falling. Calling his name. When I arrived at the forest's edge, there he was, sitting proudly, loudly, on a rusted truck shell. He was extremely happy. I snatched him off his perch and staggered back to the house, still crying. He was purring. Suddenly I wanted him there.

*

My mind became quieter as Linus began to turn to me for small courtesies: acknowledging his skills in hunting, appreciating his daily gifts of corpsicles, and rubbing his yellow tummy where his dark stripes converged into polka dots.

One night the power went out. It was out for two days. Minus twenty-five degrees during the day, so low at night that the knots were exploding out of the wood framing. Too exhausted to be afraid, I pulled my chair up to the woodstove, balanced my feet on a log, and began to eat a bowl of ice cream. Sitting close to the airtight was the only time that winter I felt warm enough for that treat. This is how I discovered that not only did Linus enjoy cuddles, rocketing around the world and sleeping the length of me inside our minus five degree sleeping bag—he loved ice cream. I also discovered that he was polydactyl. And a thief. I leaned back, smiled at him, and he, stretching up as if for a head rub, snatched the spoon right out of my hand and proceeded to slurp, snuffle, and inhale everything that it contained.

Linus hurled himself into his new life. He was free! He was safe! He was loved.

He would grab my pencil and wave it in the air: *Stop writing! I alone exist in this moment!*

I brushed his hair once. After that he would see me brushing my own and run to me, demanding that I give the brush to him so that he might perform his own styling.

And there was hunting to be done.

Linus seized flies out of the air with his "many-fingered" paws. He ate them like chips: crunch, crunch, crunch—clean paws, start again.

The two types of indoor beings I would discourage him from eating were spiders and snakes. Not because they were poisonous (they weren't) but because I loved their company. He did try spider—his handsome face scrunched up and he spat it out disgustedly. Then glared at me: *Why didn't you stop me!* I didn't laugh. Cats like being laughed at even less than humans do.

He emptied the house of its resident mice, bringing his first mouse-prize to bed so we might share in the brilliance of his skill.

Before the end of the season, he took his work outside, onto the meadow and into the woods.

Squirrels, who had had unrestrained use of house and land as both had sat quiet for years, without human presence, were abruptly given fanged and deadly notice.

I arrived home one afternoon to find a dead squirrel on the stoop. A gift.

A week later there were two.

The next week, one, devoured except its little feet, its tail, and various internal organs which he, from that time on, regarded as rubbish: heart, liver, spleen, kidneys, stomach, and intestines.

Finally came a day of four tails, four sets of tiny feet, and four visceral puddings. Yummy. The squirrels left us for the neighbours whose cats were less thorough.

After that came birds, for which I chided him. Having cost him praise, he soon lost interest in feathered beings, except for pheasant, who were huge and mouthwatering. He continued to stalk them all the years we lived on that land, finally catching one.

Being a generous fellow, Linus shared his leftovers with a large glamorous toad who sat waiting for his supper on the stoop, and a pair of burying beetles, who lived and worked next to the woodpile. *Anaxyrus americanus americanus*: Eastern American Toad. *Nicrophorus marginatus*: the margined burying beetle. The *N. marginatus* pair declared themselves by clicking fiercely at me as I approached a small animal carcass. The corpse had been moving slowly across the yard, apparently under its own volition. The strength of these tiny beings was breathtaking.

Linus's gifts to me became gifts to our animal neighbours and to the soil beneath our feet.

He was teaching me. With his fierce embrace of life and my love for him, the wild came inside—into my heart, my mind, our home. It became what we knew.

*

If Linus were here now to give his two greatest accomplishments of those times, I think he might choose catching and eating a large, fast rabbit and surviving a coywolf attack. But I might be projecting.

He brought that rabbit into the house, meowing around it so that I wouldn't know he had anything in his mouth. He was learning too. Always learning. His purrs upon presenting this amazing catch filled the large room. Such pride! Then, mid-purr, his jaws closed on the bunny's head and shattered its skull. Blood on the floor, my bunny-loving heart sad, I scooped both Linus and his prize into my arms and with, "You and your friend can play together outside," I placed him gently on the front steps and closed the door.

The coywolf attack came late in our time in Nova Scotia. Late, late in the night. I was awake, waiting for Linus, worrying. A small sound, maybe, or instinct, and I was racing for the door, flinging it open. He was there… a tangled mess of blood and ice and salt. Crying softly, shaking uncontrollably. Sharp tooth gouges marked his head and chin. Pushing aside the thought of his head caught in someone's mouth, I gathered towels, warm water, and Linus. Clean of salt and blood, dressing on his wounds, he slept, covered, on top of a blanket-wrapped hot water bottle. I did not sleep. Twelve hours rest, several changes of hot water, and there he was—staggering down the stairs, asking to go outside. "Not a chance, laddie-me-bucko!" He settled for food and kindness.

*

Six years passed.

*

I made good friends along the shore. Music came back into my life. I gave saxophone lessons to one friend, joined a band with another. Some gave me food. All gave me strength.

I grew poorer, the well ran dry, my truck, Amadeus, died on the highway in the middle of a blizzard.

Linus and I blended. In the meadow weeds and under the old apple trees, my foraging for food mirrored his hunting. Inside our home we each knew where the other was, always, without searching.

Together. "This is dangerous," a whisper in my mind. But I refused to elaborate. I had never been that with another. Neither, I think, had he. Together with one another, with the land, with the house. Through my depression, his grace and joy. Together.

# On Xanadu Everything Was Beautiful

Mary Phyllis O'Toole

December 28, 2009. Vancouver, BC.

A few days before the new decade began, I decided to go through, sort, and organize my small apartment—a symbolic out with the old and in with the new. I began with the chest of drawers that held my handicrafts and handicraft supplies. As I removed the shelf paper and shook the drawer to remove dust, a few pages flew out from between the shelf lining and the bottom of the drawer. Thinking it was just a handicraft "to do" list, I was about to throw it out but took a quick glance at the top sheet of paper. It read "Kill Me, Please." After the shock of reading the title, I realized that it was a poem I had written late in 1977 or early 1978, over thirty years before.

At the time I wrote the poem I suffered from schizophrenia, which made it difficult for me to tell what was real and what was not. In my mind, at the time, there were two worlds, the real world that everyone experienced, and the insane world known only to me. Both of my minds were constantly battling for supremacy, debating with each other about what was real and what was not. The first verse of the poem reads:

*Kill Me, Please*

*I see visions of a beautiful white palace*
*And little children playing by a sparkling fountain*
*And a lover to take me in his arms.*

Back then, in my insane mind, there existed a planet called Xanadu. In Xanadu, there was a beautiful white palace with sparkling fountains and children playing by it and a potential suitor nearby. On Earth, there were slums, children starving, a lack of clean water, and no boyfriend. Xanadu was one planet, one country, and no wars, while Earth had many countries and many wars. The second verse of the poem goes on to say:

*These visions are gossamer, glistening webs in my mind*
*Taunting me while I live my non-existent drudge of a day*
*Every night I do the books of the hotel*
*Every day I sleep while people laugh and play*
*Each night I awaken, only to add the figures again*
*While the glistening visions dance in my head.*

Around the time I wrote the poem, I was a night auditor in a hotel, working the graveyard shift. My job was to count the cash in each register at the end of the day, which was supposed to equal the total of receipts from the restaurant and hotel rooms, and then record it. The same cash reconciliation was repeated every night. The third verse reads:

*I cannot take the bottle of pills to smash those visions*
*I can only struggle through the nights and days*
*While those visions taunt and torture*

*I can kill myself so easily*
*It is those visions I cannot kill*
*So, kill me, please.*

The clash of the two minds. In one part of my mind I believed both Xanadu and Earth existed, and the other part knew only Earth. The vision of a beautiful planet where I someday may go contrasted with the reality of Earth and created a constant turmoil in my mind. The thought that Xanadu existed made life on Earth less palatable, less livable.

Perhaps the best way to understand that clash in my mind is the following analogy. A mother, whose child has been missing for years, believes in one part of her mind that her child will someday walk through the door, while the next minute she imagines her child's mutilated body lying in the woods. The contrast in her mind is terrible and she desperately needs closure. She needs to know one way or the other what is real and what is not. And so it was with me. I needed to know one way or the other—was Xanadu real or imaginary?

A few years later, I got the answer I'd been searching for. My perfect planet was an illusion. Three-and-one-half years after I wrote the poem, I would be involuntarily committed to a psychiatric ward and the planet of Xanadu would vanish into thin air.

In 1999, I was put on a new antipsychotic drug and the "positive" symptoms, such as delusions, hallucinations, and thought disorder, disappeared. Over the next decade, the "negative" symptoms of schizophrenia, such as apathy and social withdrawal, gradually faded away.

# The Children of the Damned

Bruce Ray

I speak of a world
oh, stranger
where nothing happens
without reason
where each experience
is sharply defined
and if one falls
one has to land like a cat
on its feet.

I speak of a world
oh, brethren
where we are exiles
fallen angels
branded by our sadness
set apart from the
sweet face of grace
and condemned by our mistrust.

we live in the dark world
set apart from the world
of light where children
laugh and mothers smile
our only mother is the city
and she has disinherited
her children.

there is no good and evil here
but only the shades of grey
which is the colour of loneliness
like a sickness, it is a fever
that enters the head
and causes one to live a life
of desperation.

we hate the pity
the dreaded pity that stares
at us from the eyes
of the city dwellers
we fear it and don't understand it
turning away
to go deeper into the darkness.

In the depths of the metropolis
the dead and dying live
the stench surrounds them
of dying
like the scent of sweet alcohol.

this is purgatory
where the unwanted live
in hostels and jails
and mental institutions

the exiles of the community
the children of the damned.

do you understand me?
there is no blame here
only the facts of reality
I speak of a world, oh citizen,
that you never prayed for
but if there is a heaven
then there must be a hell.
and if some are privileged
then some must be lost
one cannot live without the other.
we are your scapegoat, oh citizen.

there is no poetry or art here
but only the greyness
like the cold hard hand of steel
it is our hunger that saves us
to be hungry is to be awake.
to live without hunger
is to sleep
as if the world did not exist
see the trees
how they reach
for something neither me or you
could understand
do plants dream of seeds?
do babies wail for milk?

some leave
some walk away
toward the light
and then they are pushed back

into the darkness
to die.

Into a pool of black
into a numbness of feeling.

we accept the dark world
as our home
and we lie, cheat, and steal
to stay alive.
when you see this dying
you look away
when you see the ugliness
you are outraged
but then you accept the lie
and you feel better
after all without the dark world
the world of light would not exist.

you see the bodies
you see the strangers
without families
or a sense of community
other than the company they keep
denizens, reavers, and painted faces
they belong to the city

and they are its children.

What a bitter fruit that is
What an unkind fact to swallow
this is the death of innocence
and the acceptance of diseased cynicism
I tell you, my friend

if there was an abyss
if there was a well of suffering
if there was a hell.
I would not live in heaven.

# to make a home within desire

Rye Orrange

I've died and come back to life more times than I can count. I've touched God and been hugged by ghosts, our spirits tangling together in a web speeding towards destruction.

The blood stain on my sheets from three months ago taunts me each day as I pull my blankets back, a cruel reminder of the demons that have made their home between my legs.

While I lie in the beds of the men I fuck, the birds outside scream in agony.

The wounds of masculinity are laid out in front of me, asking to be tended and healed; trans people bear the burden of healing the wounds of others in addition to our own.

Bottles clinking together is a sound many of us know better than we know our blood relatives. When life goes sideways, we're told to find comfort and solitude in the little things—and so we do. So I did. With that method of coping came a steady flow of mind-numbing nights accompanied by mystery bruises and lost shoes. I still shudder when I recall the sensation of cold concrete against my bare feet in the early hours of a winter morning.

When I came into consciousness on the corner of Main and Cordova that early frosty morning last December, I was damp, frozen, bloodied, and disoriented. My jacket had vanished. It was 6 a.m. and I'd been on the streets of the Downtown Eastside all night. When the pulse of a hangover and the imprint of lust feel the same on one's body, one begins to lose sight of what is true and what is imagined.

*I know that God is real, because I've been saved many times before.*

I open Grindr for the eighth time this evening. It's 11:29 p.m. on a Tuesday and I'm already three-quarters of a mickey deep.

My phone screen fills with a display of shirtless men. The diverse array of toned abs, beer bellies, manicured beards, and jockstraps that I now hold in my hand never fails to hold my attention. Midnight drunken Grindr excursions have become my nightly routine; at this point, most people question why I haven't gotten bored with the app.

In the palm of my hand, I hold the epitome of queer male sexuality. How do I describe to a group of feminist friends that I search for myself in each shirtless mirror selfie and unsolicited dick pic; that to be trans and queer and masc is a mosaic of experiences that have forced me to grapple with my own desire.

Grindr opens a portal to a world that I didn't know was real. Within it, I begin to learn a language that I'm not sure I'll ever master. As messages flood my inbox, I quickly learn that I am an object of both desire and disgust; an opening to be explored.

Drifting in and out of reality, I allow men to consume me whole, hungry for what they don't have, craving what they believe I can provide.

As I find home in the shadows at the end of the world, I search for a sense of safety. That queer masculinity comes naturally to me is a lie I've always told myself. If I learn by observation, I'll observe by lying still while they break me open and discover the person hiding underneath. To be a man, or so

I've been taught, is to be afraid of what you'll find when you dig too deep beneath the surface.

# *dreaming with ghosts*

Yong Nan Kim

*our memories of memories*
*of stories*

moonlit tree
sways in the wind
shadows climb in through the window
air is suddenly sucked out of my dark room
i am not asleep
but jolted awake
shut my eyes tight
my father's ghost
touches my left arm
my grandmother's ghost
touches my right arm
their hands send electric currents
their warmth
as i remember since childhood
my body falls asleep
i am a ghost in my dream
i am in the nakdong river
i saw from a mountain
where my maternal grandfather was buried

it is silent
and deserted
i am standing alone
in crystal clear water
i can see the sandy bottom
want to go to the other side
to the third margin
walk for three days
with the ghosts of ancestors
i see mother and father on the side of the living
don't want me to go before they do
don't want me to go too far don't want me to get lost
so i wake up
after three days

i have gone too far sometimes
in busan, korea
i disappeared for a day at age 4
it was just a long walk with a friend
she wanted to go look for her older sister
we climbed a long staircase
walked and walked along a highway
at dusk i got tired, wanted to turn around
but my friend didn't want to
i came home alone
to a house full of relatives and angry parents
i told them the truth
i was not lost
grandmother was the only one who believed me

father laughed and cried a lot when he got drunk
he had many yelling matches with the ghosts of his past
they were his invisible people
we children never got to meet

we assumed that only the dead could be ghosts
during the monsoon season
he didn't want to go to sleep
as if he didn't want to go alone
to dream
when
trees
swayed
in the rain

in one of his recurring dreams
dog demon haunted him
sometimes a sad-eyed dog asked him *why did you abandon me?*
demon dogs cried and laughed at him every night
many nights a red-eyed dog chased him down and ate him

garden exorcism, busan, korea, 1970s
grandmother commands father to kneel down
she burns small nests of herbs
on his head
on his bare back along the spine
she shouts
*come out you demons!*
*in the name of jesus*
*amen!*

father never saw the dog demon again
he sobered up after the exorcism
but mother was upset with the burns on top of his head and back
she didn't want us children watching the ceremony
she said it's quackery
but i fervently believed in grandmother

in my 20s i traveled to korea
to bring grandmother to the u.s.

her visit was a dream come true for all my family
at age 91 she was still formidable and lovely as i remembered her

busan, korea,1970s
four granddaughters
listen to grandmother's folktales
every night
they would wake her up
when she drifted to sleep in the middle of a word
she couldn't fall asleep until the last one
fell asleep

in one of her stories
a girl climbs
moonlit trees
swaying in the wind
a wolf climbing
climbing,
invited to devour her whole

i have gone too far sometimes
downed hundreds of pills with a bottle of whiskey
was comatose for 3 days

in grandmother's prophetic dreams
she could see ghosts and spirits
the pig spirit showed her the fortune ahead
the tree spirits confirmed her prayers were heard
once she saw a demon
come through our front door and into my room

i was afraid she knew i had a secret american boyfriend
she exorcized me the same way as she did
when i was a child in busan, korea

alone at the threshold
i look out the kitchen door
ghosts shuffle back and forth in the backyard
awaken from their daydream
see me
smile
they are about to say something

i wake up to the bustling sounds of my house
nobody believes me
but all the doors are shut and locked
grandmother sees them too
commands the shadows
beats, drums them out of my back
then lightning strikes head to toe
i weep as hard lumps ease out of my lungs

days before grandmother passed away
i dream with my grandmother
her face glows like the full moon
she says *i'm not dead yet!*
my one song year
every morning
i sang of a small canoe
white
origami boat
no sails no oars
floating
in the blue nebula of the full moon
the face of grandmother

# Autobiography of My Grandmother's Hands (1900–1998)

Yong Nan Kim

Her hands hold a bible in the dim candlelight at dawn. Her index finger underlines each word. Leaves invisible marks. Her fingertip kissed by agape, love. Her hands come together in prayer to the god of the american missionaries. Her hands close the bible after she memorizes her favorite psalms. Her hands should be empty of books when she leaves home. The communist soldiers take away the hands that hold them. Burn them, hands and books.

Her hands grow and sell bean sprouts at the market in winter. Her three sons' hands are freezing, but she can't afford to have heat for them. The sprouts can't survive the cold. It is better to be cold than starve. Her hands long to touch her husband's absent hands. His hands are somewhere in harbin, china, where his second wife's hands warm his. His hands hold bottomless glasses of liquor and pipes for opium. His hands are empty when he visits his sons.

Her cold hands are bare when she's accused of selling sprouts without the permission of local japanese colonial authorities. Her hands are shackled even though it is after august 15, 1945. The day of liberation for all korean hands, their names, their mother tongue finally unshackled after decades of silencing. Her hands are bleeding. Swollen, and full of punctures. Her hands are mangled by a hammer in the japanese torture chamber.

Her hands take north korean refugees across the 38th parallel walking at night. Her hands manage to take a cow along. But the south korean soldiers arrest her. Accuse her of spying for north korea and confiscate the cow. Her hands are tortured. Fingernails pulled out. But one night, sympathetic hands of a guard unlock her cell so she can escape.

Her hands brush and braid her long wavy hair morning and night. Her hands get stained black when she dyes her hair because she doesn't want to look old. Her hands take out her dentures and brush them at night. Her hands hide rings, necklaces, watches, anything shiny. All kept in the treasure pouch that her hands sew into the old blankets in the attic.

Her hands ache to hold her little sisters and her parents left behind in the north. For almost fifty years after the korean war, her hands count days and nights. Collect more gifts she wants to take to her family. Her hands ache to touch her family's trees, parents' trees, three little sisters' trees, three younger brothers' trees, even if what remains in the family orchard were only burnt trees. Her hands ache while waiting for one day, someday, the days that never come. The ache keeps her hopes alive. Her hands are screaming loudly in silence. Their scars and crooked fingers have stories to tell. But they are silent.

Her hands are gone, buried far away from her mother, father, and sisters. But the phantom pain persists. As if her hands are still alive in mine.

# Home Birth

Pari Mokradi

## I

"Four years?" Dida exclaims, her eyes widening as my sister Pia reveals the news.

"I know it's a long time," I reply, though I've wanted to leave India for as long as I can remember. Canada had become *the* dream, a golden opportunity to escape the claustrophobic familiarity of my hometown closing in around me. With the visa now approved, it was the reality of leaving that somehow weighed heavy on my chest.

"No time at all, Jai!" Dida says. Sensing my unease, she turns to my sister. "After all Pia, what did I teach you both about time?"

"It's made up!" Pia repeats the lesson we heard countless times in our childhood.

"Hmm, and who made it up?"

"Pr-a-na?" we say in unison, the word conjuring up the same mysticism Dida infused into our bedtime tales.

"But you never told us how," Pia reminds Dida.

"Well, now that you're both old enough," Dida contemplates before continuing, "it all started with the very first thought in the Universe."

"The first thought?" I ask.

"Indeed Jai, the very first."

"What was it?"

Her big brown eyes catch a spark. "Desire."

"A thought of desire?"

"Yes, desire appears like a whisper, and caresses Prana. Prana cannot resist. Who could?" Dida giggles. "Prana entwines, entangles itself with desire, and from that entanglement, time and space are born. Soon bodies arrive to fill the vastness of space, and with time, more bodies, more and even more!"

"But Dida, it doesn't work like that," I interrupt, waving my biology textbook. "Our bodies come from cells, which multiply into flesh."

Dida clicks her tongue. "Prana comes first. Time, space, and everything else only emerge in Prana's wake. Where Prana flows, flesh thickens."

## II

Our steps whisper in viscous mud, squelching down the riverbank. We walk past a Brahmin priest who sits cross-legged in solemn meditation by the river, its waters reflecting the pink hues of dawn.

"I wish Pia was here," Ma sighs. "She would've wanted to immerse Dida's ashes too."

"Didi stayed with us as long as she could," I say, reminding her how my sister remained at home to care for our grandmother, Dida, instead of moving in with her in-laws, as is the tradition after marriage.

"It's just horrible timing," Ma mutters. "You came all the way from Vancouver for the wedding, and then your Dida…" She trails off, the unspoken words lingering between us. "I know these last few days haven't been easy for you, with all these rituals."

Ma is speaking of Didi's wedding as well as the night before, when we carried Dida's body on a bed of jasmine, to the burning ghats, the air thick with sandalwood smoke as we navigated around stacked logs. Dida was laid gently on the pyre, the crematorium priests working with quiet precision, chanting Vedic prayers as the fire consumed her. They then gathered the ashes into a bronze urn, sealing it with red cloth. Following the cremation, Didi left for her in-laws' while we returned home, only to leave again for today's immersion ceremony.

The Brahmin priest recites the ancient Gayatri Mantra, invoking the solar deity with a nasal and resonant voice. Sanskrit chants ripple through the liquid glow of morning air, mingling with the laughter of teenage boys bathing waist-deep at the river's edge. Ma gazes at the vast expanse of the Ganges, the sacred river flowing with a calm, commanding presence. As Dida's ashes gently slip through Ma's fingers into the holy Ganges, she says this moment should bring closure, that it should hold great meaning. There is only quiet inside me.

## III

I glance around my cramped room, where I live in the Downtown Eastside of Vancouver. The only door to the hallway is splintered at the edges, its base coated with dried waves of dirt from the last time sprinklers flash-flooded the unit. The bed is pressed against the peeling wall, and my black suitcase is wedged underneath, one corner jutting out. Ma's voice crackles in disjointed bursts as she details the cyclone that may be causing the disruption in our video call. I try to convey that my android has been unbearably slow too.

"Pia stopped by today,<br>just before the rains swept the city."

"How is Didi?
She hasn't exactly
opened up to me about her health."

"The pregnancy has not been easy for her,
I pack her nutritious lunches when I can.
Hope you're cooking healthy meals also?"

I consider explaining how my brick building was once a low-rent hotel in the city's early days. How the only kitchen in the building is two floors up, and lugging my pots and pans up the stairs always feels odd, followed by the usual "guess the smell" game. Yesterday, it was a suspicious blend of burnt popcorn and soured milk. Then there's a moment of suspense as I peek in, hoping to find the kitchen empty and, if I'm lucky, a stove that won't start smoking the moment I turn it on.

"It's fine, Ma, I'm cooking," I say,
hoping she won't ask anything more.

"Pia has been eating my boiled spinach,
just like I did when you were in my belly.
You came out with a thick head of black hair,
the nurses said you looked like a model!"

I force a chuckle
"I thought they said I'd be a footballer?"

"No, no, that was Dr. Lahiri.
Because you kicked so much in my belly!
God bless that man, if it weren't for him…"

"I know, Ma. I couldn't come out,
so he had to perform an emergency C-section.
I've heard the story before."

"Dr. Lahiri saved us," she smiles.
"You know, later he held you
while you slept, said
you just didn't want to leave the womb."

**IV**

I sit across from the counselor, watching grey light seep through the blinds with a waterlogged dampness. There have been showers across Vancouver all week and I tell Dr. M. how my mind has felt a similar grey lately, drained of color, even on the clear days.

"Most days, the clouds never part," I murmur to myself. Dr. M. makes a note and once again suggests a pill meant to help with my feelings of depression. She asks why I refuse it.

"It's just… I'd rather go through it if I can." I recall the time my grandmother bound her calves with a rope while we sat on the floor watching TV. She said the pressure eased the throbbing in her legs and let her skip the painkiller, so she could save that for when she really needed it. As she unwrapped the rope, I saw her pale skin patterned with deep red grooves.

"It sounds like your grandmother's way of managing pain left a strong impression on you. She found meaning in enduring it. Do you think this has influenced how you approach your pain?"

I consider the question. It wasn't just Dida. Growing up, I saw a lot of this in my family. Suffering wasn't something to avoid but almost a rite of passage. Sacrifice, and struggle… were markers of progress.

Dr. M. nods, "It's hard to separate growth from hardship when that's the only way you've seen it done. But there's also strength in knowing when to let go of pain."

I nod as she reassures me it's completely fine to take things at my own pace. She then asks if I've been keeping up with the prescribed walks.

"Yes, they've helped. I try to walk more often when it doesn't rain."

"Good. And the journal?"

"I am writing."

"Wonderful!"

To manage her expectations, perhaps mine as well, I quickly admit that most days I'm too tired to write. She suggests it need not be a lot—just a simple record of the day, a memory, even a brief conversation.

"Like this one?" I ask.

## V

I had reassured myself that it was entirely the pandemic's fault that I was tethered to a part-time job that scarcely acknowledged the concept of a work-life balance. Amidst the lockdown, the call centre provided me with a telecaller setup and mandated that I continue to serve customers from home. Days and nights blurred together within the confines of my small room, the only consolation: I still had a job. This also meant I had new tax forms to decipher:

Size of work space and home

* **Designated work space (room) in your home** (required)

How to calculate a designated work space (room) in your home ⑦

0 ft²

* **Total finished area of your home** (required)

What is included in the total finished area ⑦

0 ft²

## Summary of calculated space

**0 square feet** of designated work space

÷ **0 square feet** of total finished area

= **0%** of your home used as a work space and for employment purposes

The percentage of your designated work space (room) used for employment-use is **100%**, that will be used on expenses claimed for the work space only (e.g. maintenance).

Although my dwelling was branded in online listings as "***Affordable Micro Units of DTES!***" no mention was made of the size of the unit, which I later learned was called a Single Room Occupancy, or SRO. In my previous basement room, the landlord had issued a renoviction notice during the COVID rent freeze and frequently barged in under the guise of planning renovations. I spent days on antiseptic buses, yellow tape cordoning off seats for physical distancing, in a desperate search for a new home.

When I finally found a vacancy, the size didn't matter, nor did the shared washrooms. The unit had no sink and the mini-fridge barely cooled, to which the property manager only shrugged dismissively, telling me to "just follow the signs for Cold Beer in the neighbourhood." What offered hope was that I could stand and stretch my fingers all the way to the ceiling without touching it. There was also a window that looked out onto a maple tree. It was a symbol of Canada I'd come to know well from the endless reams of IRCC paperwork stamped with its leaf. I learned that maples have a unique trait in which their blood-red flowers bloom before the leaves appear. A single tree can bear male, female, or a mix of both flower types, which is why two maples can look so different during the flowering season. I signed on the dotted line. The promise of watching this tree's branches burst with ruby-red flowers before sprouting a sea of emerald-green maple leaves offered a new palette for my life, one to be savoured at a gentler pace.

Instead, Downtown Eastside life smashed through the window with jarring dissonance. Ambulances and fire engines pierced the air with their wailing sirens while buses at the stop outside beeped every half hour like a rogue alarm clock. On weekends, the streets were packed with boisterous teenagers swarming between Gastown bars and nearby parkades, their howls and shrieks echoing as they stampeded past the folks living in tents on the sidewalks.

Just as I wasn't made privy to any of this during the ten-minute showing on a quiet Monday morning, I wasn't advised of the square footage of my "micro" unit. Without a measuring tape, I used my height as a makeshift yardstick. Lying down flat by the room's corner, I inhaled dust that rose in tiny clouds from gaps between the fissured hardwood floors. Musty particles clung to the back of my throat as I stretched to mark a unit of length with my body. Memories flashed of Dondi Kata, a religious tradition I would glimpse through curtains as a child in India.

Every year, streams of devotees would immerse themselves in the sacred Ganges before prostrating along the road all the way to a temple shrine. Lying down with outstretched fingers, they would stand up, only to lie back down again. They repeated this for miles in the scorching summer heat. The asphalt sizzled as fellow congregants doused the devotees with buckets of cool water while chanting prayers for encouragement. If the grueling pilgrimage was ultimately completed, Dondi Kata was said to manifest the devotee's *heart desires*. I rose, lay back down, and repeated, measuring the SRO from wall to wall.

* **Total finished area of your home** (required)

What is included in the total finished area ?

85 ft²

## VI

The last cigarette trembles between my lips as I dodge puddles in the DTES back alley. The sharp stench of urine rises around my feet, pools with the night's steady drizzle, pattering along the path to Chinatown's Lakshmi Mart. Lakshmi, the Hindu deity of good fortune often depicted sitting on a pristine lotus flower, is nowhere to be found near the rundown corner mart, its faded yellow-and-red signboard flickering under a faulty tubelight. The entrance, with its rough splinters, is plastered with notices of missing women. The details of where they were last seen, and what they were wearing, accompany their worn-out mugshots, their eyes staring out into the bleak night.

I head straight to the cashier, grab a king-size carton of Belmonts, and light up as soon as I step outside, the deep inhale calming my nerves. Waiting for the rain to ease, I reflect on how my body, too, has been weathering a storm lately. Sharp gusts of nicotine start my mornings, followed by turbulent tides of caffeine. Evenings bring floods of THC to wash me into amnesia, while a four-pack at night drowns the incessant buzzing within my cells. It feels like a bridge is straining under relentless weight inside me, groaning and creaking. Its cables whip down the corridors of my middle school in India, unleashing memories of the empty washroom that witnessed the first beedi I rolled with my friends. The dried temburni leaf delicately wrapped the sun-dried tobacco, the quick spark insisting a deep inhale by the window. The ethereal smoke performed miracles, clearing away the debris of our perceived troubles. This high school ritual turned to rapture when we graduated to cigarettes, sold as "singles" from the corner shop. The nicotine was sharp, carving our minds into a focused clarity while our bodies flushed out the anxieties of looming exams. Soon, we lit up for celebrations too, or in anticipation of new Bollywood releases, savouring each drag just like the heroes who'd flick their ashes with flair. Somewhere between smuggling beedis down the hallways of my high school to staggering down DTES alleyways of Chinatown, escape revealed itself as an anchor.

## VII

"I'm feeling better," I tell Dr. M at my next appointment. "The world doesn't feel as washed out as it did before." Dr. M. smiles as she notes my progress. There's still one more week before I move up to the full dose.

Alongside medication, Dr. M. explains the importance of building a support system.

I describe how my network is limited to the flickering bars on my phone, which is now even dropping the video calls from my family, my primary support. And with Pia's difficult pregnancy keeping Ma at the hospital, I've been missing more of these exchanges.

"I'm worried about the birth."

Dr. M. reminds me to focus on what I can control and says it's a good sign that I'm starting to notice what's happening around me. "You are more attentive in today's session."

She's right. Just yesterday, on the bus home, I noticed the vivid orange of a man's woollen beanie, standing out in a way things haven't for a long time. It's as if the grey filter is lifting, bit by bit, and that scares me.

“I was used to the grey,” I explain to Dr. M. “It dulled the highs… and the lows.”

“Safety is complicated,” she says. She tells me how sheltering can help avoid discomfort, but how too much shelter can also close us off, making us feel isolated, even trapped. “Stepping out, even a little, can help.”

## VIII

I walk to the Stanley Park Seawall, part of the world’s longest waterfront path. As I pass through Lumberman’s Arch, I remember how these lands were once home to the First Nations village—X̱wáýx̱way—a name that roughly translates to “masked dance performance.” For over three thousand years, First Nations families lived here in longhouses built from massive cedar posts and slabs, their lives intertwined with the rhythms of this very space.

:*What about the dances in our village, Jai? Do you remember?*:

What village, Dida?

:*Where I raised your mother. You were born in the city, but she brought you to our village*:

When?

:*You were a baby, just a few months old. Our masked dancers came to bless you*:
The masked dancers? Yes, I remember Ma told me about their dancing.

:*They were dancing when you were born*:

Fresh snow powders the blue mountains like icing sugar, while the wet dapples the smaller hills of North Vancouver with lush green. I settle on a damp seawall bench, sharing the space with a seagull perched on a granite block, both of us overlooking the inlet waters.

With a flicker of curiosity, the seagull's beady eyes occasionally meet mine. Its mottled feathers are shades of wood and ash, like Dida's funeral pyre after the flames had burned low. The priest helped me rake her ashes later that evening, pointing out the fragments of hip bone that often survive the cremation. Dida frequently spoke of her hip pain, describing its ache as a stubborn companion throbbing in the stillness of night, insisting on its eternal presence. As the priest placed the bone fragments into the urn, I wondered if they felt stripped of flesh and purpose, no longer a source of pain. Or did I inherit the hurt with her ashes, the ache gravitating into me, just as I gravitated toward X̱wáýx̱way, where home was stolen and burnt to the ground?

Why did they dance, Dida?

:*It's a way of communicating for us, Jai. Not many see it as such, but if you know the language, and you do know it, you can hear us, you can hear me*:

I wish I could see them dance now.

:*You can, Jai. They are still there in our village. Your village*:

## IX

I am jolted awake at four in the morning by my phone vibrating in a frenzy. Ma's eyes glisten with worry and relief, expecting silence, now grateful for my voice. With little sleep, I stammer with weariness.

"A-a-re you okay?"

Her video feed is pixelated in some frames, the hallways behind shifting, revealing glimpses of nurses and medical equipment in what appears to be a hospital emergency ward.

"Where are you?" I ask.

"Pia...is..re…not..se..te..re..cu..n..sa.."

"What? Ma, can you hear me?"

"Yes..ve..ter..ca..y..is…sh..pr..se..res..pa...."

"I can't hear you. Where is Pia?
Where is the baby…?" I pause.

Ma's hands tremble as she struggles to steady her phone. I try to decipher her words but her face pixelates further, before freezing entirely. A notification appears on my device.

*You are dangerously low on space.*

I end the call and frantically redial, but it won't connect—*You are dangerously low on space.* I curse under my breath and restart my phone, but the message blinks back at me—*You are dangerously low on space.*

Minutes stretch as I dive into my photo gallery, my fingers tapping at a trembling pace, deleting photos, videos, audio—deleting, deleting, deleting. As the phone reboots, I look outside my window to the bare silhouette of the maple tree against the eerie stillness of the night. The empty streets hold their breath, broken occasionally by the honks of Canadian geese passing through the dark. Finally, the phone vibrates back to life, and I quickly call her back. This time, it isn't Ma's face that greets me. The image is still pixelated, but I can make out a tiny body. As the camera inches closer, I see translucent cheeks tinged with pink, delicate webs of purple and green capillaries on eyelids, fluttering.

"It's a girl!" Ma exclaims. She turns the camera to Pia, who is asleep, her hair tousled and her forehead glistening. Transparent tubes snake from her nose to the out-of-frame machines, rhythmically hissing out her vitals.

"How is Didi?" I ask.

"The baby is premature, but the doctor said they will recover just fine," Ma points the camera at the gentle rise and fall of the newborn's tightly bundled-up body. With a giggle, Ma adds, "This one couldn't wait to come out."

"Look here!" I call out to the baby, watching her eyes wander around the room. As she searches for my voice, a quiet pang settles in me, the distance between us crystallizing into the familiar ache that has shaped my life since I left home.

But then, the baby's eyes meet the camera, and I find myself staring into her big brown eyes. An unexpected warmth overwhelms me, her gaze igniting a deep sense of pride. Our eyes dance across time and space, bridging our two worlds with a delicate, renewed connection.

Dawn breaks with the thunderous rattling of the Canadian Pacific Rail engine, echoing through my DTES neighbourhood, as a flock of sparrows descends onto the tree outside. Their rapturous trilling draws my attention to the branches, yet to leaf. For the first time, I notice clusters of maple buds dotting the limbs, gleaming against the first light. Like brown skin pricked by a thousand needles, the maple tree oozes droplets of crimson pearls.

# *ache by the bottle*

Neko Smart

*after Michael Lee's "The Pill"*

the pill abets the
mind. the pill is a
sea scrubbed clean

of salt. the pill rearranges
the silence. pillages
the sound

settles into the
stomach with a
cotton mouth &

crossbow. the pill is
a softness &
a stranger to

softness. she catches at
my margins. she wears
my face or the

promise of it. the pill
percolates in red
paint. the way

sadness startles at
its own memory.
i plunder myself

of person & place until
i am no longer home
but a reminder of

home. nails over nightstand
& boots imbedded
in garden

relics of lives lost
in the dirt. lift shovel
& the pill sinks into

song or the suggestion of
song. worries herself
into rhythm. into a

chorus to kick in or
kick up or throw up.
the pill a quiet

vengeance. an indecent
tenant. little girl
of impasse &

illusion. sloughing
out ache by the
bottle. how she

rattles like a gutful
of nickel. claims
space by

burying herself
beneath it. she longs
to be a part of

something. the earth
or the idea of earth.
untouched by

lack or light the
pill is the pill is
the pill passing

through the palm. hands
bent to sky or what
is left of it

# *everything inverted*

Neko Smart

spirit halloween's mechanical skeleton has a friendlier face
than me. a lady of finery in fishnets. why bother dressing up
the dead? i envision bodies metastasized into more bodies.
a brigade of bone over bone. once i was a saint. once i was
celestial. give me a moon to hold & a sky to uncloak. i'm not
afraid of water or wreckage. my lungs give out & my ceiling
opens. my insides rattle like a caged mouth. we fuck & decide
it means nothing. everything is an inversion of itself. i live
with mould & it mobilises me. breathe through my obstinance.
i don't need a new body, only to refurbish the old one. am i
ocean enough for you? i raise the dead when i raise my
voice. call when i'm lonely & am greeted by my own breath.
i learn to live underwater & am, in effect, learning to live.
this brain is a reluctant host. i've fumbled its biggest bolts.
the chimney is leaking. the foundation is flaking. i'm ghosting
out safe words, but there isn't a syllable to stave off the flood.

# EyeTap

Quin Martins

Philip Morgan stands in his darkroom, inspecting his freshly developed prints that hang from clothespins. The pungent, gasoline-like smell of the developing chemicals fills the air, and the amber-red safelight casts a warm glow. The darkroom's silence is his sanctuary, grounding him in the present moment.

A rarity among photographers today, Philip insists on shooting exclusively in film. For him, this is more than a preference—it is a vital part of his artistic philosophy. He feels the medium captures moments with a depth and richness that digital photography can never match. And, like other analogue photography enthusiasts, he believes in the value of the artifact—having something real in his hands to hold.

As a street photographer with an anxiety disorder, Philip's routine consists of engaging with the world in short bursts and then retreating to his cocoon, his darkroom, to find solace from the external chaos. Today, however, even his safe space doesn't feel safe.

Philip's thoughts keep returning to this morning's video call with his daughter, Iris. Like most twenty-four-year-olds these days, Iris is a whiz with anything tech-related. Eager to support her dad's career, she constantly encourages him to promote his work online. But Philip worries about losing creative control over his images. Not surprisingly, he was completely caught off-guard by Iris's call this morning.

*"So, dad, you finally did it. You decided to upload your photos to the internet."*

*"What are you talking about?"*

*"Those prints you showed me last weekend in your darkroom—I saw them posted on EyeTap."*

*"What the fuck is EyeTap?"*

*"It's a new social media app."*

He could not believe his eyes when Iris shared her screen to show him his unedited photos posted online for all the world to see.

*"This can't be happening!"* Philip cried out, his sense of reality unravelling. *"I haven't even scanned the negatives! I feel like a character in one of those dystopian science fiction stories by… that Vancouver author whose name I can never remember!"*

*

Determined to get to the bottom of how her father's unscanned photos ended up on the internet, Iris dons her virtual headset and begins her research. Immersed in the digital landscape, she skillfully navigates a myriad of publications, forums, and websites to discover a company named EXISTech, which is at the heart of the mystery. The trail of digital breadcrumbs she follows leads her directly to Steve Mann, the enigmatic owner of EXISTech and the EyeTap app.

As Iris delves deeper into his history, she learns that Steve Mann is no ordinary entrepreneur. His relentless pursuit to merge the physical and virtual worlds has not only pushed the boundaries of cutting-edge technology but has also sparked ethical debates about privacy, surveillance, and the human-machine interface.

EXISTech, under his leadership, has become a powerhouse in the tech industry, specializing in wearable computing and advanced digital imaging technology.

Excited to share her news, Iris calls her father.

"Dad, I've found the firm that makes EyeTap, and it just so happens that they have an office building downtown."

"Excellent," Philip nods, grateful for his daughter's support. "Let's go there right now."

"Okay. Meet me at the Grind on Main. I'll tell you more about what I've learned and then we can head over together."

*

Philip sits hunched over his table in the crowded coffee shop, waiting for his daughter to arrive. "I hate this place, it's always so fucking busy," he murmurs to himself. He would have rather met at one of the cafes on the West Side with the automated servers, but he knows how much Iris cherishes The Grind—one of the few traditional coffee shops remaining in the neighbourhood.

The sweet and sour aroma of freshly ground coffee permeates the air. The sound of young people tapping away loudly on keyboards is drowned out by the racket of a coffee grinder, while rock music by musicians long dead plays over the stereo speakers.

Feeling self-conscious sitting alone, he punches up an article on his screen. The article, "Dignity in Detritus—The Street Photography of Philip Morgan," is a favourable review from a local arts magazine of an exhibition he had in the early 2000s. He'd probably read it a thousand times, but ever since a recent eye operation, he's had trouble with his vision. As a photographer, Philip's eyes are his most important asset. His art is his life and he's dedicated decades to perfecting his craft. His doctor reassured him that it was a routine procedure, but something went wrong.

Philip strains his eyes to read the letters on his screen, but they are blurry and words appear to be shifting at the corners of his eyes. *1N d1GN1TY 1N d3Tr1tus, 5TR33T PH0T0GR4PH3R pH1L1P m0RG4n PR353NT5 4N 3V0C4T1V3 V1Su4l 5TUDY OF THE C1TY'5 H0M3L355 TH4T 1S B0TH 1NTIM4T3 4ND C0NFR0NT4T10N4L. kN0WN FOR H15 ST4RK BL4CK-4ND-WH1T3 PH0T0GR4PHY, m0RG4N UT1L1Z3S F1LM T0 R3FL3CT TH3 P4SS1NG N4TUR3 0F B0TH TH3 SUBJ3CTS' L1V3S 4ND TH3 PUBL1C'S 0FT3N FL33T1NG 4CKN0WL3DGM3NT 0F TH31R 3X1ST3NC3…*

Philip bangs his device down in frustration, startling the woman beside him. As soon as he looks up, he spots his daughter's turquoise-dyed hair bouncing through the crowd towards him.

"Finally!" Philip grunts, when Iris arrives at the table.

"What's wrong?" she asks.

"Nothing. My eyes are bugging me. It feels as if I have a bug stuck in the corner of my eye that I can't get out."

"I'm sorry dad, that sounds awful."

"Ah, forget it. I don't want to talk about it." God, he hated his daughter to see him like this. Anxious to change the subject, he asks her what she's learned about EyeTap.

After Iris fills him in on her findings, Philip sits in stunned silence for a moment, his brow furrowed as he tries to process everything. Then he abruptly jumps up from the table.

"Okay, let's go!"

*

Philip and Iris head towards the city centre, where EXISTech's headquarters loom large, a monolith of glass and steel. Philip scans the environment, unable to shake the feeling that someone is watching them. Upon arrival at EXISTech's imposing offices, they are greeted by a sleek, robotic attendant.

"Welcome to EXISTech. How may I assist you today?"

"I need to speak to someone about how my photographs got posted on your website without my permission!" Philip answers sharply, his fists clenched.

The robotic attendant's eyes flicker. "I'm sorry, I do not understand your request. Can you please r-r-rephrase your question?"

Philip and Iris exchange uneasy glances. After a moment, a young woman emerges from behind a curtain, blushing. "Sorry about that. We're still trying to iron the bugs out. I see that you have an appointment with Mr. Mann. Please proceed to the 139th floor."

"How did they know we were coming?" Iris whispers.

"I don't know, but let's go," Philip answers, his determination growing.

As the elevator ascends rapidly, Philip's mind races with possibilities. *How the hell could they have gotten their hands on my photographs?* It's not the monetization of his art that bothers him so much as the violation of his artistic integrity.

At the 139th floor, the pair exit the elevator into a giant open space. From a distance, a tall, skinny, balding man waves them to a large desk. "Mr. Morgan, Ms. Morgan, welcome. I have been expecting you," Mann says, a faint smile on his lips. "Please have a seat. Can I get you something to drink?"

"Let's cut the bullshit! Tell me how my photographs ended up on your website without my permission," Philip demands.

Mann once again gestures for them to sit. "It's a bit complicated, but I assure you, it's not as nefarious as you might think."

Philip and Iris hesitantly take a seat in two plush office chairs.

"Mr. Morgan, Ms. Morgan, have you ever heard of the term *Humanistic Intelligence*?"

"Yes," replies Iris, "I remember reading about it in my research. Humanistic Intelligence is a feedback loop between a computer and a human being, where the human and computer are intertwined."

"Very well put, Ms. Morgan. Over the past five years, EXISTech, with the help of our team of volunteers, has been developing a form of Humanistic Intelligence. Using wearable computing, we can tap, if you will, into the volunteer's vision. Hence the name *EyeTap*."

Momentarily, the room falls silent as Philip and Iris absorb what Mann has said.

Mann breaks the silence, "Mr. Morgan, did you happen to undergo eye surgery in the past few years?"

"Yes, I did. Why do you ask?"

"Do you remember being asked to sign an agreement before your operation?"

"Yes, I do. But I never agreed to this!"

"Have you ever heard the expression that you should always read the fine print? I venture to say that this advice applies here," Mann quips, grinning.

"So, you're telling me that ever since my surgery, you've been stealing my vision?!"

"Here at EXISTech, we do not like to use the term stealing. We prefer to consider our arrangement a collaboration between us and the volunteer. Think of this as an opportunity to share your work with the public. Finally, millions of people—our EyeTap users—can see the beauty you create and bring to the world!"

"You mean you can monetize me by selling my artistic vision to the world!"

"Mr. Morgan, I am not doing this for the money. I have more money than I could spend in ten lifetimes. Our mission here at EXISTech is to create the world's first fully integrated human-computer interface, and you are helping us realize that goal," explains Mann.

Unable to contain his rage, Philip jumps from his seat and overturns Mann's desk, its contents crashing to the floor.

"Mr. Morgan, there is no need to make a scene. I would rather not have to call security."

Iris grabs her father's hand and pulls him towards the elevator. "Dad, let's get out of here. There's nothing we can do."

"Fuck you, you digital demon!" Philip yells back at Mann as the elevator doors close.

Outside the building, Iris consoles her father as he sits on the curb, crying, his hands covering his face. "It's okay, Dad. We'll get through this," she says.

"What do you mean *we*? I'm the one who's going to have to live the rest of my days with a computer chip lodged behind my eyes!" Philip sobs.

The two sit in silence, dejected. When Philip looks up, he catches a glimpse of sunlight reflecting off the window of a nearby skyscraper, and the silhouette of an eagle circling overhead with its wings stretched wide. A smile creeps over his tear-soaked face.

"Wow, that would have made a beautiful photograph."

# The Box

Jean Kavanagh

The box is 30 centimetres by 23 centimetres by 23.5 centimetres, off-white and brown cardboard with a snugly fitting lid. Its contents were disappointing from the start.

Heavy for its size, the box contains my hospital records on about 500 sheets of 8.5 x 11 paper, mostly doctors' and nurses' notes, pharmacy requisitions and emergency room entries. It seemed like a good idea when I learned that patients of St. Paul's Hospital in downtown Vancouver could receive their records free of charge. (I'm glad they were free because it's hard to imagine anyone wanting to pay for such memories.)

*

A decade before I requested the records, I'd experienced a year of long hospitalizations for depression. It took me that long to garner the courage to ask for them. I'd hoped the pages would shed light on details of my four, two, and one month hospital stays. I told my psychiatrist about a year after what I refer to as "my year from hell" that I was considering obtaining my hospital records. He looked aghast.

"I'm not sure that's a good idea," he said, sitting across from me in his outpatient office. "I think it's too soon. Maybe in a few years."

I took his advice until I could no longer ignore the hope that accessing the records might help lift the veil on my illness. I wanted to know what the doctors thought had caused the worst depression I had ever experienced and why they went as far as to recommend and administer shock treatment—yes, like in *One Flew Over the Cuckoo's Nest*—to treat it.

What would this medical history say about me? Maybe if the records were about cardiac disease or MS or cancer or some other "acceptable" disease it would be ok. But I had a mental illness—severe depression. What would these pages reveal about my illness? Would I learn anything? Why did I think getting these records was important?

*

The process of requesting my records was easy. You filled in a form on St. Paul's website. Then someone called when your records were ready, and you arranged to pick up your box. My box. Filled, I hoped, with diagnosis information and treatment details to augment my hazy memories—being taken to an operating room, telling my story to revolving classes of medical students, staring out the window to Burrard Street for hours at a time. Some images came to the foreground, like when you develop photos the old-fashioned way in a bath of chemicals that slowly brings forth the picture. This might be a way for me to fill in some blanks, I thought. I hoped the pages would answer questions, help make sense of what had been a senseless year.

*

About a month after requesting my records, I received a phone call to inform me they were ready. I was surprised at the butterflies I felt as I approached the records department on St. Paul's Hospital's main floor. A young woman greeted me with a smile, went through a door to retrieve my box, and wished me well. Because of its weight I had to carry it close to my chest, but I was able to take it on the bus. It wasn't big or heavy enough to require a cab. I opened the box as soon as I got home, and after reading the first page—dated September 8, 2015—I learned the contents contained "a copy of the complete clinical records you requested. These are produced in accordance with the Freedom of Information and Protection of Privacy Act of British Columbia." The pages included my Daily Medication Administration Records (a lot of those) and contact information should I need further assistance.

The feeling of disappointment was immediate. The first pages were mostly sheets of medication records (I guess you do take a lot of medication during long hospital stays), illegible doctors' notes, and a few typed "consultation reports." Not much insightful information. My hopes sank. After leafing through about 50 pages, I closed the box for six years.

*

Six years after pushing the small box to the back of a cupboard, I pulled it out again. I'd decided to try to write about that year and about what led up to it. This time, I went beyond the first 50 pages, reading all 500ish. I had hoped for insight, not just a record of medications and my daily mood on a scale from zero to ten. There were only a few references to ECT, or electroconvulsive "shock" therapy, the most dramatic of my treatments both personally and medically.

About a month into my first hospitalization, doctors began to talk to me about ECT when medication wasn't doing the trick.

Days before receiving my first treatment, I remember sitting in a tiny office, literally closet-sized, on St. Paul's Two North ward with a young doctor who'd taken over my care when my older inpatient doctor was away. The room held only his desk and two chairs. My back touched the wall.

"You know what the only option is?" he said in a low voice.

Wrapped in my housecoat, one of the few things I'd brought from home (along with my pillow and a small Bodum coffee pot) for what was turning into a long hospital stay, I knew what option he was referring to.

I had been stunned when the doctors first suggested ECT, but they assured me it wasn't like in *One Flew Over the Cuckoo's Nest* anymore. Much research had been done to refine and tailor the treatment specifically for a patient's needs, they told me. Feeling pathetic, and no doubt looking so, I slowly nodded my head, agreeing with the doctor that at this point it was probably the only option.

I had originally thought I'd come to hospital for a few weeks and get better, since, much as I'd tried to shake what was the deepest depression I'd ever had, nothing worked. Not my dance class, not running, not gardening, not trying to be with friends—I just wanted to disappear. Anxious to be well again, I was like someone trying to get into a luxury resort, calling St. Paul's daily for over a week until they finally had a bed for me. But once in the hospital, things got worse, and now I was facing shock therapy.

My brother, Liam, had come from Calgary to be with me. When I told him what the doctor, who never actually uttered the words, said about ECT, we looked at each other, rather lost, and agreed that maybe I should try it as it does work for some people.

I'd met a doctor in the hospital—a patient who was a physician, not someone working there—as well as an artist and mother of four who said it was the only thing that worked for them. The doctor came from Vernon, in the British Columbian interior, where he lived and worked. He came to St. Paul's every six months, depressed or not, for what he called a "tune up." Getting those synapses firing correctly and avoiding falling into a deep depression when he'd be of no use to his young family or patients. The artist's latest hospitalization was before her son's wedding—again, preventative. She knew it would be a stressful time and stress was one of her triggers. So, even before she bought her mother-of-the-groom dress and shoes, and before she made hair and make-up appointments, she made a visit to St. Paul's Hospital's Two North ward. With those examples for reassurance, I signed the papers and the next morning was prepped and taken down to a basement operating room for the treatment. When I awoke, I couldn't remember my name or where I was.

Before the second session, a nurse suggested that I write my name and "St. Paul's Hospital, Vancouver" on a piece of paper so that I'd know who, and where, I was when I woke up. So, in the chicken scratch my handwriting had become because of the various medications I was on, I took her advice and the note was taped to the cabinet beside my bed. After the second treatment, I actually remembered my name, but the chicken scratch was handy for locating where I was.

The notes about ECT in my hospital records include:

> *"ECT in A.M. Very disoriented afterwards and distressed. Unable to recognize where she was, time of year. Needs reassurance that this loss is temporary."*
> *"Has to make herself a bedside sign for post ECT reorientation."*
> *"Short-term memory remains very impaired, as far back as six months."*

The doctors had thought that two to four sessions would help fix me. After the sixth I said I didn't want to do any more.

The depression hadn't lifted, and there were large gaps in my short-term memory. My long-term memory was intact. I knew where I was born, who my parents were, and what and where I had studied, but memories of the preceding six or so months were gone. A friend, trying to be helpful, said that might not be a bad thing.

Over the years when I was a patient at St. Paul's, both in the hospital and out, my in-hospital doctor was a lovely kind man in his sixties. He was away at the time of the shock therapy experiment. A few months later I sat in his office on the psychiatric ward, and as he reviewed my file, he shook his head. "Well, no wonder it didn't work. They didn't take you off all of your meds."

The doctors who treated me hadn't followed this protocol. Now and again on Two North, I used to see the young doctor who had recommended the shock therapy, and I felt he was avoiding me, eyes down, never acknowledging me when we passed each other in the hallway. Even after I left the hospital, I often thought of speaking to him about it but never did.

Medication has kept me from falling into the depths of depression I experienced thirty years ago. But it's been so hard to accept that this is an illness and not a character flaw. Stigma is real.

# The Devil You Know

Justyna Krol

The break happened at the beginning of March, after an extended winter. It was the kind of March that leaves ruts of slush not just on the roads but spilling over onto the sidewalks, turning everything grey and watery. The girl had left school early to go to the dentist, which felt like a reprieve at the time—a way to escape the humiliations of gym class—but now, with her face stiff from the drilling, she didn't feel like she had gotten away with anything. The filling would later turn out to have been shoddy, at least according to the silver-haired university dentist who redid it a few years later, but this dentist was Polish, and therefore could be trusted not to "rob us blind," which is what had mattered to the girl's mother.

The girl decided to walk home rather than take the bus. She hoped that there might be some beauty to be found in all those shades of slate along the sky and road. The girl needed awe, something to haul her brain out of the pit it had been digging, full of thoughts having to do with the fact that she should not be here, not in this place, not even within the grand scheme of things.

It didn't help.

As hard as she looked she couldn't find anything to catch her eye. Once the freezing rain started she was finished. She was living inside a pathetic fallacy. The greyness of the weather felt deliberate, a living thing determined to drown her. As a child, she had once read a fairy tale about a malevolent spirit, a waifish man covered in dark green slime who would pull his victims into a liquid, murky death. She felt like another one of his victims.

When she finally made it home (she couldn't remember how) the girl laid down on her bed—her clothes wet and cold—and cried for hours. She didn't know why, and when her parents asked what made her so miserable, all she could say was "everything" while staring at the ceiling. Her younger sister sat with her for a while, then left and returned with a piece of bread. The girl took it, holding it as she would a tissue. She got up eventually, ate the bread, drank tea, pretended to be a person. She lasted another two months. When she couldn't bear it any longer she bought sleeping pills from two different pharmacies and swallowed them all. Her parents found her drowsing in the bathtub, full of pills and grape soda, still trying to shake the cold. She was admitted to the psychiatric ward that evening, a week before her eighteenth birthday.

*

When they had first immigrated, the girl and her sister did not find the town grey at all. They arrived in March, but a different March altogether, one with flowers and warm breezes and birds they had never seen before, and all the chocolate and canned pineapple the girl could eat (she loved the canned pineapple almost as much as the chocolate). Things looked promising. And even though she missed her old apartment and her sixteen first cousins and her father's library, she loved the stores with their full shelves, the sharpness of her new clothes, and the shine of the kitchen appliances. The pop-up toaster, in and of itself, was a revelation. Besides, her father told her that they wouldn't be staying here forever but would be going back home once her mother's contract at the university was over. The girl didn't realize that this was not her mother's plan, because if she had known, she would have packed more books.

And so their exile unfurled. The girl's parents had a series of drawn-out fights that her mother—as always—had won, or at least dragged the fight out enough to outlast their visitor's visas, and thus long enough to ensure they couldn't return to Poland at all (at least not if they wanted their old lives back without the threat of imprisonment, after what had clearly become an attempt at defection).

It was during these fights that the girl first found her knack for dissociation. She didn't know what to call this thing that had happened to her at the time, coming across the definition when she was decades past being a girl. She discovered that, somehow, she had managed to complete the process her family had started—she had emigrated from both her home and her body. Was this the opposite of possession? Did it still count if you were the one ceding your own self, even without any willing takers? Still, the girl could finally get far enough away to erase her own memory, far enough to forget the yelling, to forget her mother's complaints about the girl's unwillingness to fit into her new school, her reluctance to go outside into the new, overwhelming world.

Later, her mother told her how, in the middle of one of the fights, the girl had started coughing violently. She even started to shake. This made her parents stop long enough to make sure their eldest daughter was okay before resuming the battle. The girl was startled by her own actions in this retelling. She was bolder in absence than she had ever been in presence.

This strange amnesia was a relief. It was a wonder.

It was almost as useful as getting lost inside a book, but without the residual story to contend with (unless someone insisted on filling you in later). Maybe they were true, all those fantastic tales of the old west she had read in Polish translation as a child. They had been about America, but wasn't Canada close enough? Maybe this was a place for reinvention, a place where who you once were disintegrated in the face of what the new country needed you to become.

By the time they brought her to the hospital after the pill incident, the books the girl had brought with her when they immigrated had been read and reread dozens of times. She had long since moved on to English novels far more advanced than her compendium of fairy tales and Polish folk legends, her translation of the adventures of Dr. Doolittle and his animal menagerie. But at the hospital reading proper books had become near impossible, which was harder to bear than almost anything else, harder even than the loss of her taste for pineapple and chocolate.

Her emotional break, which had started as a fissure on a freezing March afternoon, was now a canyon, and it was impossible to imagine ever getting back across. Her mother told the girl to pray, told her that she herself was praying every day for her daughter's hospital release. That was fine, her mother could do what she wanted. None of it felt relevant to her situation. She didn't care where she was. The hospital didn't make her feel better, or safe, though that was how the ward's admitting nurse had described the psychiatric unit. Considering that the first nurse she met, the one that rushed her in to have her stomach pumped, spent what time they had together to tell the girl how she was wasting everyone's time and taking doctors away from the real patients, the girl's sense of safety was just one more thing that wasn't working as intended.

And the schedule of the place!

The staff assigned her so many tasks, all of them endless, exhausting, impossible. Taking a shower: impossible. Not just the getting up, the undressing, and the lathering, but withstanding the assault of the pressurized water on skin required more dissociation than the girl could pull off. Participating in group therapy: impossible. When trying to talk, she felt like she was operating a wooden ventriloquist's dummy, the doll being her own body, the puppeteer unskilled. Sleep: okay, possible, but just barely. And even when it did come, it left her bereft at five in the morning, an especially cruel time as she had never been a morning person, not even as a baby, when—according to her mother—she had slept later than any other infant and cried pitifully if woken too early.

Still, there was sometimes a brief respite that could be found, every two days or so, very late in the night, when the girl's brain was tired enough to abandon its fixation with her unworthiness, ugliness, freakishness—"Why are you so abnormal?" the girl's mother had cried during her last visit, that word "abnormal," so cutting in Polish, a real brand, a stigmata, nothing like its clinical English counterpart. During those moments of respite, she would pick up one of her old books, the one filled with old legends, entitled *The Lives and Times of Polish Devils*, and find herself almost lulled.

Not that she imagined any kinship with the demons. She did sometimes feel like she caused evil things to happen, ripping her own family apart by the sheer misfortune of her existence. But the girl had always imagined real evil as something that had the benefit of high self-regard, which she herself had not been cursed with (pun absolutely intended). But the devils as described in her book were nothing like the biblical demons she heard about when she attended English churches. They were more like slightly supernatural beings who stumbled around the earth with greater or lesser skill and better or worse intentions, trying to find ways to curry favour with hell's high council in order to eventually be allowed to make their way back home. This was the bit that resonated because she too wanted to get back home, to her previous "normal" self. Maybe she could switch places with one of the devils? They wanted to get back to hell and she wanted to get out. They should talk.

*

When the girl had been an even smaller girl, she had floundered under the expectations of goodness. To be a Good Girl was to be a respectful girl, was to be a brave girl, was to be a forthright girl. And yes, discovering the WASPy, Anglo-Saxon version of the Good Girl was a surprise. Sure, the well-mannered part was still there, and the physical modesty it implied, but the rest of it—the gracious, opinionless vacuity—that was new, and not any easier to master. Good Girl status was an elusive goal to aspire to. It wasn't even that the goal posts kept moving, it was more like they lacked the clear boundaries that a goal required. How can you get the ball in the net when you can't tell where the net is and isn't?

In Poland, where things were at least familiar, the "right thing to do" was less confusing but could still be fraught. She remembered a time when her father asked her to fetch him his cigarettes. The girl loved her father and wanted to do what he asked. But she had also just read that smoking was very bad for you. She did not want to scold her father the way her mother did, to tell him he was wrong to want what he wanted. How should a person carry out such a request? The only way she could: the girl handed her father the cigarettes. She said "Please don't smoke too many."

Things grew only more complicated. Even being a loner did not guarantee you could escape the discomfort of conflict. One time, when the girl was walking home from school, an older student followed her home. He walked a few meters behind her, singing all the while about boys and girls hugging and taking each other's clothes off. The song made her skin crawl. Each time she saw this boy, dread filled her and congealed her voice, making it a stopper pushed deep into her throat, solid and tight. After the third time it happened, she decided to tell her mother. "What was he singing exactly?" her mother asked as she furiously scrubbed out the tub in preparation for her younger sister's bath. The girl had trouble explaining. It felt like if she repeated the song to her mother she would be letting it contaminate her, making everything that happened her own fault. She did her best though. She muttered, "boys and girls," "naked," "hugging." Her mother laughed. "You dummy. Just tell him to beat it. You can't expect anything to change if you don't speak up." The girl stood there a while longer watching the sponge scour away the grey smudges left behind by soaking laundry. Her mother's Virgin Mary medallion glinted back and forth as she worked, a silver eye blinking. The next day, the girl waited in the school bathroom long after the last bell, and then took a different route home.

*

Lying in her hospital bed, the girl reread the story of Hejdasz, hell's most inept servant. Hejdasz was a devil so stupid that instead of feeding the condemned souls under his watch molten lead and hot coals, he served them moonshine and roast pork. After he was kicked out of hell by Lucifer himself, he wandered the earth failing to ruin, seduce, or damn anyone. He wouldn't even try to hide his devilish appearance. Instead, he decorated his horns with flowers and brushed out the tuft of his tail until it shone. Though Hejdasz took real joy in his own appearance, no one else was impressed. People mocked him for imagining his horns and tail to be beautiful, and other devils denounced him for not disguising himself in the service of deception and temptation.

The girl had always liked Hejdasz.

It occurred to her that this demon had a better idea of what it was like to live as a teenage girl, and an immigrant, than anyone else she knew. He understood what it felt like to navigate your own existence, physical and otherwise—to the approval of no one—while still hoping one day you could return to some simpler time and place. This, of course, was never going to happen, not for either of them (she knew this story inside and out, and Hejdasz wasn't going home anytime soon).

She closed the book feeling the familiar aggravated exhaustion return. It was dark outside, but there was always enough light coming in from the hospital's corridors to read by. Her roommate—an elderly Portuguese woman suffering from Alzheimer's who was waiting to be admitted into a long-term care facility—was snoring away. Here they were, the beginning and the end, lying side by side, and neither one with a brain she could trust. The girl felt tears threatening and her throat trying to choke them down. She was bored of tears. They never made anything better. She got up and quietly scuffed her way to the bathroom. Turning on the tap, which always ran hot no matter what you did with the knob, she cupped her hands underneath it and drank.

Her hands and tongue scalded.

It was strange, really, the way all the mundane things they asked of her—the teeth-brushing and hair-combing—brought nothing but agony, but this, the burning pain of the hot water down her throat, this felt like a relief. Her molars with their still new fillings ached at the change of temperature. Her throat blistered. She thought of Hejdasz and his prisoners. If she had been one of his charges, she would have refused the moonshine and taken the molten lead. She would have drunk it all and asked for seconds. This was something she could do, this was something she had always done. And she wanted it to mean something, a sacrifice of one devil for another. Maybe one of them would get to go home. Maybe one of them could stay safe.

# *To be a child is to try*

Justyna Krol

again, again
they tell you, and so you tell yourself, try
and maneuver a thousand things
outside of your control:
the traffic on the way to school,
the itch of your plaid pants
                    (you would have never chosen plaid,
                    but trying is not the same as choosing)
the drunks staggering from the hedged field
squinting into your line of sight
hurry, try, disappear
into the vague distance of their hangovers
into the gate
the classroom
the corral of expectation.

survive what you can. try
to remember your lunch.
get through the long hallway
and make it to the bathroom in time
to the music still in your head from

those shows your parents
won't let you watch so you let them
sing you to sleep from a distance.
you have no allies here,
but you have the hum of your memory.
try to invent what you need.

try to return
to your small bedroom after a long day
in a world too large for your purposes
and place, on a narrow ledge, a stone
you picked up on your way home
a button you'd rather keep than wear,
the three books a harried librarian let you take.
then, walk through your day
as you have arranged it,
the moments collected, unmastered, but here
open to interpretation
small enough for the hold of your hands
like the pieces of a board game
you will try to play
again, tomorrow.

# I was asked for advice, once

Justyna Krol

See—this is beautiful too:
the way you go over your childhood failures

        and these—the failures, the body
        (only one of you getting older)

Swoon—like the stem's certain dip, like a slowing,
the allotment of pulls: all this gravity

Love—the way that your casings will loosen
your surfaces wend, lean unreliable

Listen—I too thought there would be time when I would not
reach for my father or mother

        but time does not diminish lack
        only absence,

Still—I wanted to tell you
about the time I became, till I lost the plot

Look—I broke and unbroke
all that: and no narrative arc

So be—this hour,
however it takes you

Praise—your worn-out digestion,
the slick rot of autumn, the cries

        of crows, war-deep in a carcass
        and tear your want from their want

Then scrap—be fought over, sullied,
be known, for all it was worth.

# As someone with ADHD, I will never build a spite house

Justyna Krol

*"In 1925, a wife agreed to divorce her husband on the condition he build her an exact duplicate of the home they shared in town. Because she didn't specify where the house should go, he built it where it would cause her the most unhappiness: [on Plum Island] by itself, far from everything, no fresh running water (only salt). There's a term for this: 'spite house.'"*—Kate Bolick, "Plum Island's Pink House Inspires a Real Estate Fantasy," *New York Times,* Dec. 11, 2015

*"Thanks to the Second Gulf War, America has become the official enemy of the state. At the entrance to the five-star al-Rashid hotel, Saddam has had a huge mosaic floor laid, featuring the face of former American president George Bush Sr. … Here in the Middle East, to strike someone with the sole of your shoe is a sign of disdain. This mosaic induces everyone passing through the hotel to tread all over the former president's face."*—Karim M. S. Al-Zubaidi, *Iraq a Complicated State: Iraq's Freedom War*

Sure,
I have nurtured grudges,
as you would a small animal, faltering
I have polished the sphere of my anger
and burnished it to a bright white gold.

With a fury of movement I have hurled
hatred, pain, or defiance
and thrust my own hands deep
into the furrows of malice.

Still,
finding rough tracks is my nature—
what I lack is commitment, grit,
held reins for a real showing

So,
I could not build remotely on Plum Island.

My first step would halt me, make me watch
the salt marsh brim with itself and days
would pass before I remembered the blueprint
or fathom why hate
should earn you such beauty.

Instead,
I would embroider my disdain with metaphors
or the sign language of angry drivers, but not
crosshatch my ill will into a portrait
of you, my enemy
and tile your grin to the floor
for my feet to strike again and again
in cacophonies of contempt.

The flesh is willing
but the spirit is weak—
my deficits don't stop at the state of my closet
but burst free into worlds, where
they can forget their rash purpose
and return to their constant searching
for a straw in the haystack, where
the flickering sameness burgeons
much more than the sting of anomaly.

Now,
lost in the grass I forget
whatever it was that I came for:
revenge, forgiveness, this four-leaf clover?

Instead I'm brought to my knees by the tangle of growth,
and remember the earth as it stood once
rich with indolence, indifference—
my life before you made me this mad.

# A Faulty Compass

Christy Frisken

Lying in the dark at 4:30 a.m., I'm anchored to the mocking pain of the accruement of old injuries—landing on my hip playing frisbee, falling off my bike near Spanish Banks (the gravel was so loose, so dry), slipping down the wet cement steps outside a friend's apartment building. Unable to shift my body weight without a sharp, needling jolt down my spine, it strikes me that I am stuck in the grips of the past. My body refuses to let me forget my clumsiness or my choices.

*4:30 in the morning is the hour many people get out of bed to pray or meditate*, a kind doctor once mentioned after I told her I didn't want to take sleep medication for my insomnia. Meditation could be a decent analgesic. Maybe I could pray and grow closer to God.

Instead, I twist my shoulder deeper into my mattress and hope that helps. I can't disconnect the word God from my discomfort in the church I attended as a child, or its wooden pews vibrating softly with my father's conspicuous snoring, or the thin, earnest voice of my mother. Her singing voice did not match her speaking voice. Using the word God feels disingenuous and it reminds me of my shame.

I don't remember the Bible verses my mother quoted at the breakfast table, but I recall that I tried to sit quietly, my eyes pinned to my cereal bowl in case I was caught looking at my older sister, who was easily set off. I didn't understand what my mother was teaching us, or why it felt so urgent, and I felt as though there was separateness between me and this God. God knows everything, but my questions for God extended far beyond the verses she shot in my direction—*rat a tat tat!*—though my imagination seemed to marry anxiety to my historical trajectory. I was an object to be talked to. I wasn't a real person. I could be thrown away for objecting, or for not complying.

We were Not Like Other Families. This, I learned very young. We didn't socialize much during the years we attended church as a family, and we didn't socialize, ever, after we left. Dad's family was overseas in a country we'd never visited. Mom hadn't spoken to her sisters in decades, yet she talked about them constantly, always in unfavourable terms. *This one is a nut. This one is a horrible person. This one's husband beats her. This one's husband sleeps on the couch in a sleeping bag and keeps porno magazines on the coffee table, in full view.*

The last funeral my mother attended was her father's, held a few months after I was born. *You slept through the whole thing*, she told me. Hearing that I slept so well as a baby, as a child, even as a teenager, proved to me that I was capable of doing something right. My champion sleeping didn't last though. I don't know what happened to me. Insomnia set in when I was thirty-five and didn't abate. I do know what happened to me. I just don't know how to talk about it.

*

When I was a child, my family's faulty compass pointed away from the forward direction other families faced—we faced backwards into the past, but never my own past. Everyone knew everything about me already. I couldn't hold their interest. While other families looked forward to day trips to the lake, with cousins visiting from back east, family barbeques, and vacations to Disneyland, I faced my old relatives through the lens of history.

As a teenager, I never thought of family in nostalgic terms. Never. We moved frequently enough for me to feel traumatized. The displacement was painful. I missed my old friends, good times, past successes, and even the kids who always, always had more than me.

Being poor hurt my self-worth because I was too naïve to realize that money wasn't everything. I was afraid of the future. Teachers spoke of college and degrees, jobs and careers and RRSPs, marriage and children, and houses with mortgages. The idea of it—any of it—terrified me. As if worrying about hell and damnation and Satan wasn't enough. When I was sixteen, I left school and then I left home. Once I was out of the house, I left religion behind and made my break from God. I met unsavoury, low-life people who lived as though the apocalypse was coming for real, but this time I thoroughly enjoyed it. These people, especially women behaving badly with me as their witness, helped me out of my abyss.

*

I wondered if she still lived in her old place on 18th Avenue, the top half of a house planted within a city block of multi-family dwellings. We hadn't spoken in several years, not since she turned up on my doorstep, three years after she ended our friendship. She rang the bell until my partner answered the door, then asked that I come downstairs to talk to her *before I lose my nerve*. I didn't know why she'd come, or demanded that I speak to her right this moment, but I wouldn't.

I was in the bath when she showed up, soaking away a memory held in my shoulder—it had been twisted abruptly while I tried to hold back an old friend who was determined to throw a bicycle at her boyfriend. I refused to get out of the bath. Still too angry, I asked him to tell her I was unavailable. He came back up to tell me *she said this is a one shot deal.* I slapped the bath water. *I am in the bath!* I was like a toddler. My partner suggested that maybe she wanted to apologize and reminded me of the decades we were so close. *Why would she show up and tell me to drop everything, or that's that? Why does she get to control everything?*

I called her several days later, annoyed that her phone number was burned in my memory. We met for coffee.

*You are so angry*, she said, her tone surprised, as if nothing could have ever been wrong to begin with.

*You threw me away like I was trash*, I responded, willing myself not to cry. *I don't even know what I did to you. I was there for you, for years and years, any time you needed me, I was there. You suddenly cut me out of your life, with no explanation.* She had no recollection of this. Perhaps it was the combination of time, stress, multiple injuries, and the fog of addiction. Her bewilderment at my anger and her inability to recall what transpired between us hurt more than her ending our friendship did. I couldn't bear sitting beside her.

*I need to go*, I told her.

*Okay*, she said. She didn't seem bothered, and I hated that.

There was no apology. There could be no resolution. Nearly twenty years of sisterhood, gone.

*

For years after our coffee meeting, I tracked her through her Craigslist posts, which always included the intersection closest to her house. I regularly visited the website to reassure myself that even if we were no longer friends, at least I knew that she was alive, and I knew where she was.

Her posting style and her proclivity for flipping Scandinavian furniture and housewares gave her away. Some of her pieces never sold, like the Norwegian container the colour of motor oil spilled on water. Her things were priced for other obsessive people with niche interests. The container was listed on Craigslist for what felt like years. In my mind's eye, I could still see it on the shelf above her guest room dresser.

On Craigslist, we were still friends. I could type her intersection into the search bar and review what she was selling. The green wool sofa her son and I both claimed was too itchy. Solo teak chairs from the collection I knew she kept in her garage. Shoes and scarves that had me wondering where she wore them. She'd once told me that an ex-boyfriend used to respond to her ads with crude propositions. *Want to fuck?* I thought of him when I thought of responding to her ads. *Can we talk?*

So, I went to take a look. I stood across the street from her house for a few minutes, hesitating. I took a deep breath and crossed 18th Avenue like I was crossing the Rubicon. There was a disco ball hanging in the window. Multi-coloured bottles queued along the sill, cheerful and inspiring though they appeared, convinced me she had most definitely moved. A disco ball was not her aesthetic. There was a single steel post driven in the grass, resolute. The tetherball post. Her son was nine years old when they moved in. He spent hours playing by himself until one day the chain and ball simply vanished. Ten years after our friendship ended, I stood outside her house, staring at the barren post. The air was absolutely still but my heart kept fluttering. The Craigslist ads remained in place, but she was gone.

# Our First Names Started With the Letter J

Jaki Eisman

You pinged my radar, right away, as someone to avoid.

So I sought you out.

I was 29, still young enough to believe in sprinting towards any jagged cliff that beckoned.

We did have a lot in common beyond broken brains and storied childhoods. We were loners, homebodies, TV devotees—we took to solitude like irreligious monks. We were novice writers, and your literary gifts—those glowing first drafts—thrilled and annoyed me, depending on the day. Our first names started with the letter J, like characters in a nursery rhyme.

We worked at the same office building, you as a self-described "*Good Will Hunting* janitor" (you were a cleaner) and I as the assistant of someone's assistant (I made photocopies). We met on the carpeted hallways that you vacuumed, became fast friends at the Xerox machine. We bitched about our coworkers, called them "normies," as in normal, as in *not like us.*

People found us weird and we knew it. But out-weirding each other? Our number one pastime.

*

We were different from each other, too. You were ten years older and a whole foot taller than me, and your height, dark eyes, and flat affect conjured Anthony Perkins in *Psycho*. I felt like a bit of a *Bambi* when with you, but an edgier *Bambi*, that liked dark skies and horror films.

On the first walk we took together, you told me about your single mother. About how, when you were little, she had you take photos of her in a wet t-shirt she gave as gifts to her boyfriends. You told me that you drank most nights, that you kept a beer-brewing vat in your apartment which made the tiny place smell like yeast. You sometimes hired sex workers, not for the sex but for the company to drink with.

You had no filter to speak of.

I told you that I had no friends.

Words were easier than touch, and we kept things platonic. We were emotionally scarred, sexually ambiguous. When our shoulders brushed by accident we pulled away as if burned. We found safety, instead, in our late night phone calls. You called me from your offsite cleaning gigs—once from a bird hospital—and we talked about our pasts, our jobs, our tastes in music and TV, our shared true crime obsession. You were sympathetic to serial killers, blaming their "mother wounds" for whatever came next.

"But we all have mother wounds," I argued. "And we don't all go around killing people!"

"Don't we, though? Don't we? Murder takes many forms."

Huh.

Huh?

*

I may have been an assistant's assistant, but since our workplace was unionised, I moved up in the world. Or at least I moved into an apartment where the kitchen and bedroom were not *the same room*. On my thirtieth birthday, I invited you over, and you showed up bearing gifts: a case of cherry beer that looked like cough syrup and a box of spongy Chinese dumplings you planned to steam.

It was summer, and outside was a bushy green tree plucked straight from a fairy tale. I put on the *Jesus Christ Superstar* soundtrack—we both liked it, not in an ironic way—and smoked a cigarette by the open window. You sat cross-legged on the couch, held an unlit cigarette and pretended to smoke it. "The only thing better than smoking is not smoking," you said in a faux-British accent, riffing on a famous Noel Coward quote.

Then we sat together and sang to the music between sips of the over-sweet beer. I was wearing a scoop-neck top, neck and collarbone on full display, and you stared hard. As your pupils dilated, your eyes grew blacker than usual.

"You have a nice neck. Pale and slender."

*

I let the wrong one in.

I always do.

I always *did*.

Before wising up.

Before wising up and shutting the door and bolting the lock and wedging a chair under the door knob for good measure.

Now? I let no one in.

And wonder: which is worse?

*

In monster lore, vampires can't enter homes unless they've been invited in.

(*On my thirtieth birthday, I invited you over*)

But, as writer Hrvoje Milakovic notes in *Fiction Horizon*, "it's not just about entering homes. This rule reflects the idea that evil, represented by the vampire, can't harm you unless you allow it to. It's a choice, an act of free will. By inviting a vampire in, you're metaphorically (and, in this case, literally) letting darkness into your life."

I let the wrong one in.

*

"Up for a birthday throttle?"

There it was: your absurdist sense of humour. Or so I assumed. A birthday throttle? Things with you were always weird.

The summer birds chirped outside, and I was tipsy from the beer. So I offered my neck in mock-submission. "Ooo… yes please!"

I thought you were joking, so I joked right back. I thought we were friends. But your face: stony, hard. Your eyes: empty, unblinking. Your hands: big, strong, and wrapped around my neck. Squeezing tighter, tighter, tighter. Stars swimming in my vision.

*What's happening? What are you doing?*

The corners of your mouth turned up, a sadistic half-smile. I'd seen that face before, in all the gory 1980s horror flicks I watched in my youth. Through my shock and my fear it dawned on me that a flirtation with the darkness was nothing compared to facing the darkness itself.

My head filled with blood. There was a thumping in my ears as the room went blurry.

*

You were diagnosed with schizophrenia in your teens, but that didn't scare me. It's a statistical fact that most people with mental illness are more likely to be the victims of violence than the perpetrators. I was hardly a beacon of stability myself—depression, obsession, etc., etc.—and mentally interesting people were my jam.

You were one of the smartest people I'd ever met. The genius janitor, straight from a movie. I wanted to believe that while the world didn't "get" you, I did.

I knew you were off-kilter—I knew you saw the world through a lens darkly. But I didn't know you hated women. Did I? Men treating women like shit is what I grew up with. Or maybe it was more nuanced than that: hurt-people hurt people, regardless of gender. Men just happen to be more physically imposing. Like you.

*

When my survival instinct kicked in, I shoved you off me, breaking your trance.

I gasped and wheezed and gulped air, trying to get as much of it into my lungs as possible. Then I leapt off the couch and grabbed the cordless phone from its cradle, trying and failing to form words.

"Out! Now!"

You didn't budge, so I held the phone dramatically, the keypad visible, and pressed the "9" and the "1" in an exaggerated manner. "If you're not gone in 30 seconds I'm pressing '1.'"

You left, and I shut the door and bolted the lock and wedged a chair in front for good measure.

Yes, your mom fucked you up. Yes, society shunned you.

But I wasn't your mom, and I definitely wasn't society.

I was like you: alone, misunderstood.

So I let the wrong one in.

# *Party Girl*

Harry McKeown

& then i stole a dress from forever 21 it was surprisingly easy i took my bag into the dressing room & i stuffed a pink dress inside i did not try on but i could tell it stretched & would flare around my hips too big & hug the curve of my abdomen which was flat enough i poured happily into the sunshine with something to wear

& i began drinking the wine in my bag on the way & it was fine because it was a student town in fact a group of boys yelled from across the street we love a party girl & john had already started drinking i changed into my dress & he had half a bottle of wine on the table & i said i'm drunk let's call connor go dancing

he poured me a glass & his face crumpled like he would cry he asked me to help him finish his wine & i did & some got on my new dress & i pulled the tag off a ragged hole appeared & i worried if people would see the flesh of my waist & he watched me drink then he asked can you tell me more about why you hate men

& then his bathroom i pressed my pink self against the floor & judy garland sang old man river from my phone & her pain thundered & i could not remember how i got there & judy's face was scared of dying & i left the bathroom my dress ruined i could tell & john sat there unmoving he said i think i understand you better now & to this day i cannot remember the rest except just keeps rollin he keeps on rolling along

# *Party Girl II*

Harry McKeown

party girl wants to be an actress. party girl blacks out with her friends every friday. party girl loves pbr because it is the cheapest way to stop feeling. i have been writing this poem for nine years. when party girl drinks, she blacks out. when she wakes up, she is trying to kill herself. dryer sheet on the floor. the smell of boiling water. i find party girl in my heart. she comes home from the boy's house. party girl finds ants on her windowsill. she boils water and pours it into the cracks of the walls. she burns the dress she was raped in. she pours into the morning with purple arms. she wants to be an actress. she will be an actress, if she tries hard enough. the wind blows through her. i have been writing this poem for nine years. i write it for party girl. for her arms, for the fire.

# Inside Screaming

Crisi Corby

Clutching the arms of the chair, knuckles white, I feel my pulse pounding in my ears as I fight to stay present. Shame is driving me from reality in this moment. I focus on the floor, imagining what I just confessed as a dark puddle growing on my sister's carpet, its surface tension weakening, ruining everything it touches as it slowly spreads. I imagine myself frantically scooping up the liquid, unable to take back what was now spilled. The crystalline darkness changes, starting to look more like blood, and I've gone from scooping to clawing, and the ever-present "inside screaming" echoes loudly in the background of my imagined struggle.

*

"I don't actually want to kill myself."

My sister looks overwhelmed with sadness.

"It's more like a tension release," I continue, anxious for a response and hoping for a sign of relief in the shadows that darken her face. "It's hard to explain." I tug my sleeves back down to cover my forearms.

I sink into the chair and lower my eyes to the floor. *God. Why am I such a piece of shit?*

It will take everything in me to look into her face again. I concentrate on her rug, avoiding the disappointment… the pity I might see there. I feel her gaze, though, burning through me. Her confusion and anguish thicken the air. My regret about my decision to tell her, to show her, makes it difficult to breathe.

To hell with it. Secret's out now. I look up.

*

The ritual, as of late, was happening more frequently. It had been almost a year since our family was rocked by a series of deaths. The most recent one was an event that intensified my ritual's obligation and drove me to a near-daily practice: an hour-long shower in scalding hot water, an ice-cold bottle of vodka for courage, and the slow, practiced bloodletting. The cuts were getting deeper, messier, and harder to hide. I was hoping that telling my sister might slow me down… give me a break from the cycle I found myself in: my bloody rite, the disdain I'd felt for feeling so out of control and needing it, and then having to rely on the ritual to relieve the disdain. I thought telling her might help us share in our grief, and maybe even temporarily quiet the near-constant, intrusive thoughts that'd been occupying my mind—the screaming that no one else could hear. I thought that telling her might even provide respite from the agony I felt over the ending of my relationship.

My partner had just broken up with me a few days earlier. That's why I was sleeping over at my sister's.

"I just don't love you anymore," he'd said.

That's hard to hear from the person you love, especially if you're under the impression that the love you shared was unconditional, though I understood why he ended it. It must've been hard to love someone who had been lost to sadness—someone who survived by disassociating. He knew about my ritual. I'd been doing it for a while by the time he dumped me.

*

My sister is wide-eyed. Still processing. Possibly in shock. I can see the tension in her face travel down her neck and arms, ending in tightly coiled fists of contained energy, like she's stopping herself from slapping some sense into me. She stares at me with delicate restraint, her mouth agape. I sense she wants to say something but is worried that the intensity of her reaction will scare me.

She finally speaks, her words clipped. "This has to stop! You've got to talk to someone." She pauses for a few seconds and takes a deep breath. Then, in a calm and measured voice, as if negotiating a hostage situation: "What are you *thinking*?!"

I thought that this would be easier to explain, that she would understand my rationale. It isn't going well. I try again.

"Sometimes, I just get so intensely overwhelmed, I get this… out-of-body desperation that drives me towards a sort of… release. It quiets what I call the 'inside screaming'… When my thoughts get to be too much, everything suddenly gets drowned out by a high-pitched tone, and then all I can focus on is the image of my face. Mouth open. Then the tone gets replaced by the sound of my screaming. Sometimes it stops on its own. Sometimes the cutting is the only thing that makes it stop. I never seem to know whether I've truly been screaming." I suddenly feel uncomfortable for baring too much. It might be more than my sister can handle.

I start to pull up my sleeve again to show her that it's not as bad as it looks and sounds. "Look, they aren't even that deep."

She flinches.

*Fuck.*

Her eyes open wider, and tears pool at her lash line. She looks terrified. Pleading. *Is she scared of me?*

This is my fear being actualized.

I don't know why I'm so scared of being misunderstood. Why am I more afraid of my loved ones thinking I'm deranged than I am of the disturbing and intrusive thoughts I've been having? My sister's reaction, though, confirms something I already knew: what I've secretly been doing to my body for years is far from rational.

In this moment, I realize that no matter how hard I try, no succinct explanation will help my sister understand the nuances of what I do. I want desperately for her to understand how my cutting is different from the self-harm depicted on TV and in movies. I'm an adult in my twenties with a career. I'm not looking for attention, and I don't think I've ever really felt like I wanted to die.

How do I truly help her understand the screaming that engulfs my thoughts? Or the ritual? How do I convince her, without sounding delusional, that this ritual is actually a good thing that stops me from doing anything worse?

I can't. I've barely scratched the surface, and she's still just… staring at me.

Instead of taking the conversation further, we do what we do best: we wrap up the too-dark conversation with half-hearted reassurances. I pledge to not cut again and to start therapy, and she tells me she feels relieved, neither of us really believing the sincerity of the other. But we are tired, so we keep it light for the rest of the sleepover, neither one of us willing to see each other completely through the darkness.

*

I watch my sister giving in to sleep beside me, undoubtedly exhausted by the difficult conversation. I wait to see her chest moving rhythmically before rolling over. Staring into the darkness, I consider, probably seriously for the first time, just how far I'd gone to rationalize my cutting ritual. At what point did it become normal to me? Precious to me? Part of who I am? I'm not an idiot. I understand that to most people, it would be shocking. Alien. To my family, it will be heartbreaking. *Crazy.*

That last thought, *that word*, echoes from the dark, murky parts of my mind and wafts out into the night air as I breathe deeply. I shiver and notice my body is less tense than earlier. The tightness in my shoulders is gone.

My thoughts return to the word "crazy," accepting its implications. Someone in my family was bound to end up with that label. In losing the people we loved, and then experiencing the grief that followed, a crack formed in our family's façade and dark family dynamics revealed themselves. I'd kept the screaming and my ritual a secret so my family wouldn't be further inconvenienced or made uncomfortable. Hiding "the crazy" had taken a toll on my sense of self and on my relationship.

My family loves my partner, so I imagine I'll have to shoulder the disappointment for everyone as he disentangles himself from our lives.

We'd been happy for a long time. But so much of what we had grew from a traumatic night when he'd been my protector. My saviour. My entire family stood behind him and loved him for it. The whole scenario created the illusion of a safe and unbreakable bond, one that I happily settled into. My protector, however, also happened to have a habit of having sex with me while I slept.

I never hated him for it though, I never told him not to. I never had the energy to consider that he shouldn't use me that way, or that I had the right to tell him "No." We just didn't acknowledge it. Everyone has secrets. He wanted to keep his secret, and I wanted to keep my ritual to myself. So, we lived together knowing we'd never address the darkest parts of ourselves with each other, that we'd never confront one another with the truth. Over time, the relationship eroded, probably from the constant strain of keeping up the fantasy of a normal partnership, and the respective self-hate we felt because of our secrets.

As I finally allow myself the space to acknowledge this, the room begins to lighten. I let the shame of it wash over me, which makes me feel a bit nauseous. But then my arms start to feel a bit lighter and my stomach relaxes. I can't figure out if the lightness I feel is because dawn is breaking, because I let myself mull over thoughts I'd kept hidden away, or because of sheer exhaustion.

*

I watch my sister breathe as she sleeps beside me. I think about how this isn't the first time in my life everything has seemed like too much for me to handle, and about how I've somehow made it through with her help. Sharing my secret could be the start of my journey out of darkness. I'm ready to let some light in and whatever change it may bring—be it a straitjacket or meds… or alienation. The shame and the pity that may come with that will be tough.

Despite looking peaceful, I know sadness is likely plaguing my sister's sleep. She doesn't realize what she's given me tonight in letting me disrupt her peace, in listening at the expense of her comfort—a sort of forced sacrifice. One that may help me finally quiet the inside screaming.

# Baby-La-La; [redacted] Un-umbilicalated[1]

jerry LaFaery

What's that old chestnut?
If it's not one thing, it's your mother.

*

Mother died, and lived, in the same spot, for all of her ninety-eight years… same house… same town… same everything.

Most of the people she knew, she had created.

Of her six children, I was the last. The birth order went like this: male, female, male, male, male, queer. Or it could also be described as: Alcoholic, Alcoholic, Lost/Mad, [redacted]p Supporter, Flat-Earther, Heathen. Or it could be, [redacted], Multi-level

[1] Parts of this fictional account have been redacted by the author, to assure anonymity and limit litigious retaliation.

Marketing Disciple, [redacted] Worshipper, Heartbroken-Child, Depressed/Sleeper, and Baby-La-La. It's impossible to sum people up in one word… it's also unfair. Other words could be applied liberally too… like conspiracy theorist, [redacted], team-player, sneak, and liar, cheat, sneaky, slippery, rageaholic, bully, devotee, artist. Although I wouldn't say my father was racist, he would more than once say, "I got all chiefs, no [redacted]."

…all shouting to anyone who would listen… but no one was.

If past lives and wishes are to be believed, then maybe I might have prayed for something like, "Oh please, in the next life let me be close to someone, and I want them to never leave me and like to cuddle close."

And WHAM! Wish granted!

I had always suspected I was conjoined to a parasitic twin, even asking my Mum directly, "Where is my twin?" This question always made her head tilt, and produced a perplexing expression on my mother's face. "Twin?" I also suspected that I most likely absorbed my twin while sharing the womb. I must have figured they were too weak to survive this world, so rather than lose them completely, I subsumed them. Together forever. To this day they are the only family member I bother much with. At least this theory would explain my extra wisdom teeth, and the third nipple behind my knee.

Eventually Mum's kids had kids, and their kids had kids… it's literally a story older than recorded time… and so everything ticked along, until she became a great-grandmother. My brother [redacted] had this idea, "I think when you get to be fifty you should start subtracting each year, so like on your fifty-first year you would actually count it as forty-nine, and keep counting down like that… that way you don't get old." At first I thought it was a joke. It wasn't until I witnessed my ten-year-old Mum relating to her great grandson, that I agreed completely with him.

Her passing gave birth to a hollowness in my family, and a further disintegration of family ties.

Having birthed four males and one female, I think Mum secretly, even secret to herself, wanted another daughter. Feeling it might level out or disperse the heavy cloud of testosterone that overwhelmed any chance of balance. Instead she got me. A non-binary queer, bent on non-assimilation… careful what you wish for I guess. When I confronted my Mum with the question of whether I was a planned child, she skirted the issue saying, "everyone was always so happy when a new baby was brought home," smiling a welcome smile, and that was the end of that.

Being raised in a remote northern Canadian pulp and paper town, on a bland diet of seventies American television sitcoms, I understand what it takes to disappear completely. If it wasn't for "centre-square" Paul Lynde,[2] I don't think I would have survived. He was the first "capital Q" queer I ever recognized, and he was on television! He was the inspiration for my drag persona, Paula-Lynde LaVeaux. The LaVeaux part comes from a New Orleans creole herbalist, midwife, and voodoo practitioner who was said to be over two hundred years old.[3]

But now, after my mother's death, I needed to be seen. I had a eulogy to deliver, and, finally, I was going to be heard.

In my eulogy I call out the stifling atmosphere I experienced while growing up homo in a small town. It was basically a big [redacted]-you letter to my place of origin and my [redacted] birth

---

[2] Reoccurring as "centre-square" guest star on the popular 1980s game show, *Hollywood Squares*, and they also appeared as the witch (the term "witch" is a gender neutral word often mistakenly referring only to women) Uncle Arthur on the American sitcom *Bewitched*.

[3] Historians point to LaVeaux's naming of all of her children and grandchildren "Marie," and dressing them in the identical costumes she wore, as a way of creating the illusion of "living forever."

family, finally letting the secrets and lies loose. I wanted to enrage them and embarrass them… shrink them into a manageable, harmless, comical size, and abandon them completely.

I had only been in drag three times before the eulogy.

*

It took a while, about twenty years or so after my father died, to not hate him so much. Paradoxically I don't really blame him, but I do. It's a complicated remembrance that can be boiled down to alcoholism, or expanded to include child poverty, mental health, [redacted]-family dysfunction… the usual.

As a break from the daily grind of tiny-Town-life, some of us would be volunteered to work on the trapline, an expanse of Canadian wilderness that I could not appreciate at the time, and which still holds some problematic memories. Here I would learn to trap and hunt and skin… but not to the degree that would make me self-sufficient, but in a piecemeal way that broke everything down to labour and work. There was very little broader understanding or meaning to what was happening. For example, we would be told we were going trapping minutes before we would leave, without a clue about what that would entail. It always felt like it took forever, and I always felt like an unnecessary addition. Dressed for the weather with my Mum's help, I would be so bundled up at points that claustrophobia would set in. Still, this was preferable to the cold of forty below.

*

Mum helped me with my very first drag performance. I was about five or so. I don't think I was even in kindergarten at that point. There was a dress-up event being held at the local playground, which my sister had been hired to manage. There were three playgrounds in total, each serving the three amalgamated communities that made up the paper company town of Pour-Qui Falls. The three towns were joined by pavement and taxes but separated by language and culture. The divisions were based on the usual stuff, including labour hierarchy, education, poverty, bosses, middle management, immigrants, French, English, and business, and farmers, and religion. We lived in the poor section, a mixture of everything… except money and power… unless you described power as brute force.

The event was very exciting, like a summer Halloween. Looking back, I can see my hopes were counting on the female energies of my family to rise up and smite the male energies down… back into their respective cages where they were free to rage and tear each other apart.

But I am an unreliable narrator when it comes to the truth, because I grew up in the same system as my oppressors, so, dear reader, it would be good to keep your wits about you. The story would be different if my siblings told it. If they had told it, they might say my eulogy was a desecration (…wait they would never use that word). My brother [redacted] might say something like, "…it's only common sense, ya don't come to a funeral dressed like that… I mean there's kids there, we don't want you shoving yer rubber lady parts and puttin' on a sex show… Gaawd… then he, she, whatever that wants to pretend it is, starts spewin' garbage, startin' with 'hey queers?'… I mean, at 'is own mother's funeral… she'd be rollin' over in'er grave."

It was an open casket. I watched her. She didn't budge.

# *It Is Ordered*

Angela J. Gray

A repetitive childhood dream

> I squeeze through the basement window. It's hard for me but I fit through the small opening. It is pitch black outside. It is not raining. Everyone is asleep upstairs in our home. It takes so long to get through the window. I wish my twin, William, was with me. I can't wake him but sleeping in the basement alone makes it easier for me to get out. I climb over one fence and then another. I finally cross over two of the backyards. I crawl through the opening in the other backyard. I cut my hand. I am bleeding. I have to keep going. Five more backyards to get through. I go this way so no one will see me. I must make sure I don't wake the dogs. When I get to Lain Road I run.

I have escaped.

If Michael does not visit me no one will know that I am gone.

Angela where are you?

Angela where did you go?

Angela?

ANGELA?

ANGELAAAAAAA.

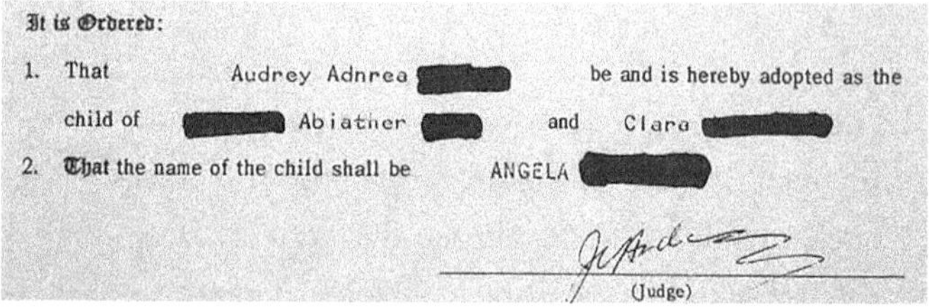

It is Ordered:

1. That Audrey Adnrea [redacted] be and is hereby adopted as the child of [redacted] Abiather [redacted] and Clara [redacted]

2. That the name of the child shall be ANGELA [redacted]

(Judge)

Angela became my name some Friday on the second of the month decades ago. It was ordered stamped and approved by Judge J.C. Anderson in his chamber. Audrey, the name my mother gave me, was lost to me for thirty years. Beside Angela, on a birth certificate tucked away, is the name of the mother who raised me. A name I hated vehemently after every punch she gave, name she called, and sorry she did not speak.

Audrey is my original name.

AND IN THE MATTER OF The Child Welfare Act, 1965

I have repeated my first name, Audrey, time and again, since I learned this is what my birth mother Dorothy named me. Angela is my accepted name. I will likely never change my name back to Audrey. Some days, when the memories are hard, I think about it.

AND IN THE MATTER OF The Child Welfare Act, 1965

AND IN THE MATTER OF The Child Welfare Act, 1965

AND IN THE MATTER OF The Child Welfare Act, 1965

AND IN THE MATTER OF The Child Welfare Act, 1965

"You must feel so grateful that your parents adopted you," people often said. The envy, admiration, and disdain of my parents' choice evident in their tone. The assumption of their thoughts not lost on me; your white parents have done you a favour.

My response: "Sure, I guess."

I have always found the weight of being chosen to be oppressive. This thick blanket of expectation was my companion every night I lived in Clara and Abiather's home. I felt obligated to behave in a way that I did not understand, because of a contract that I did not participate in creating. Even today I am reluctant to mention I was adopted.

It is Ord

It is Ord ... s Ordered:

It is Ord ... s Ordered:

*THE CHILD WELFARE ACT, 1965*

**ADOP RDER**

I began my new life crying in a highchair, in a room unfamiliar. Clara shared a story over dinner once about this time. William and I howled for the first two days we lived in our new home. She released an odd sort of chuckle while she described this. At dinner time, when my food was not yet finished, Clara often reflected on the past or doled out humiliations for punishments needed, because of something that happened in the present.

*"It was noted, after you joined your adoptive parents, that you took a while to settle, but eventually you and your brother began eating and sleeping well. Other children in the family reacted well to your arrival, playing with you and sharing their toys. They were delighted with their new sister and brother."*

My twin and I became members of our new family on Canada Day. We were officially adopted three months later. We arrived that summer before my memories were formed.

I did not settle. The siblings, who once eagerly shared their toys, became people I secretly began to dislike. When their play became nightmare-worthy, my unravelling began. I found solace in leaning my back against the cedar tree in the backyard. Today I seek the cedar tree in the yard where I live when the day is hard. I will stand beside it, allowing all that pains me to be taken away, absorbed into it. My existence in that house never made sense to me and over time I began to hate the word chosen. Trees made sense to me. They never instilled pain.

There was a sunspot near the lilac tree that bloomed every spring beside my parents' house. I loved sitting there. The smell of lilacs reminds me of that insignificant place that was safe. The sun took me in. I disappeared into it and dwelled in the quiet stories that occupied my mind. Sometimes, though, when I could not contain all that I could not speak, I would kill the ants that were close to me. The bugs that I could hurt. The killings caused me anguish. I will now, whenever possible, catch a bug if indoors and put it outside.

*

My siblings were told my absence was due to a surgery. I needed my umbilical cord removed because it hadn't fallen off properly. What I had was a bacterial infection that could not be identified. I was told the doctors burned my toys and the clothing I came into the hospital with because of this.

Clara and Abiather had directed me to look out the window and wave at my siblings. They were visiting me. I cannot remember if Susan, Michael, John, Myra, or William were there, sitting on the hood of the Chevy, while I looked out of my white, disinfected, hospital room. As I looked down from the hospital window I could see the bay where the boats sailed. I know Ann was there. Her smile, her long hair, her arm stretched higher than the others, I still recall. Ann told me not to tell and I didn't tell anyone about what she made me do to her. Clara just couldn't understand why I could not stop throwing up. I just kept throwing up until there was no choice but to take me to the hospital.

I do not know if that was the last time. I do not know how many times it happened before. I never liked seeing Ann in that blue velour housecoat. Whenever I did, my body tensed and I instantly felt bad. Whenever she pulled me down the basement stairs while wearing that housecoat I knew I would soon feel crummy. A shame I would not understand until much later in my life.

In my grade five school year Ann was away at college. I was sent to sleep in the basement. In Ann's bed—that bed. All alone, surrounded by her things. I had many night visits and nightmares that year.

Upon Reading the certificate of the Director (Director or local director) under the said Act and upon considering what was alleged by or on behalf of the said applicants and being satisfied that compliance has been made with the said Act:

My parents believe they loved and cared for me as they were tasked to do. Clara showed her caring through cooking and she was a good cook. To make holiday turkey dinners Clara rose at four in the morning to prepare a feast for nine. She would also make roast chicken, roast beef a bit too well done, and the occasional lamb meals. These meals filled our stomachs so much it was hard to move. Every night before we were sent to bed we were to eat something—toast, popcorn, or fruit. Susan, Ann, and Michael became caregivers as well. They also made sure that I was fed.

*

I attended a conference about Human Resources in my second year of college. Gloria Steinem spoke about her book *Revolution from Within: A Book of Self-Esteem*. I bought the book even though I didn't have the extra money to do so. I didn't feel good inside. I never had. More importantly I didn't know what it meant to feel good. If I was *even allowed* that. I had spent several years by this point self-medicating to manage anxiety that I never spoke to anyone about. That weekend, while my classmates stayed in the hotel where the conference was taking place, I stayed with Susan. She met me near where the conference was taking place and took me out for dinner.

"I will buy your meal. I am not paying for your alcohol," she said.

I have sketches of black and white in my mind of Susan caring for William and I when we were beginning to age out of the toddler phase. The two us in the back of the Chevy while she drove us to the sitter who was to care for us. Another time Susan cared for me while I sat in her lap, on the couch in the basement, where she *nursed* me.

**Upon Reading** the certificate of the Director (Director or local director) under the said Act and upon considering what was alleged by or on behalf of the said applicants and being satisfied that compliance has been made with the said Act:

*

I relieved my sorrow and feelings of disconnection, then, by taking solo walks with our dog, Duchess, in the wetlands behind the family home. Most walks brought pleasant memories of picking wild strawberries in the summer and cross-country skiing with Abiather, John, Myra, and William in the winter. We explored this land and the creeks that ran through it. We caught tadpoles and frogs where garter snakes dwelled. We lit fires to distract us from whatever was happening in our lives and we were yelled at for doing so. The smell of roasted crab apples still remains with me. This outdoor place was a haven where we chased imaginary grey horses. Where we tobogganed and fought with each other and other children in the neighbourhood. Where my brother John shot me with a BB gun that tore the skin off my ankle and showed a bit of bone. Another time I didn't tell.

I began to accept that my birth mother was not coming to save me and for now this was what I had. I found a way to deal with the constant knot in my stomach, and the nightmares that invaded my sleep, by excelling at school. I thought this would help Clara and Abiather accept me—see something good in me.

*The Adoption of Negro Children: A Community Approach*, a social experiment, is responsible for my adoption. This project completed with a document placed on a shelf in the York University Library. This project lost in a document on a shelf. There was no evaluation of the efficacy of the decisions the Social Planning Council of Metropolitan Toronto and the Children's Aid Society made. They said even the hard-to-adopt deserved to be loved. Did love really have something to do with it? Perhaps the goal was to get these hard-to-adopt Negro children out of care and into any home that wanted children?

### *THE CHILD WELFARE ACT, 1965*

# ADOPTION ORDER

Upon [redacted]
considering [redacted] compliance [redacted] on behalf of [redacted]

[redacted]
applicants [redacted]
considering [redacted]
[redacted] compliance [redacted]
[redacted] had been made
[redacted]

---

Credits:

1. Collage design inspired by work with Otoniya J. Okot Bitek
2. The Adoption Order for Angela J. Gray
3. Quote taken from the non-Identifying Information of Angela J. Gray
4. The social experiment document "The Adoption of Negro Children: A Community Approach" published by the Social Planning Council of Metropolitan, Toronto in 1966.

# *Journey*

Gilles Cyrenne

Was I religious
I would pray to St. Joseph
    patron of cuckolds
    God fucked his wife

I am some distance from sainthood

I thought we were negotiating
        when she moved out again

But now there's a baby daughter
Born into this world    home birth

This mother, wife, wants me to taste her breast milk
    I hate milk    always have    despite
    growing up around buckets of it
Now I'm as erect as a cow's teat
        useless as teats on a boar

"Why are you writing," she asks
"Writers don't make any money."

She dredges memories of parents and teachers defecating
on my creativity

Marriage my half-hearted attempt at normal
bombs out at beginning of nuclear family of three
I become toxic radiation
I fall out of intimacy
(do men get long postpartum depression?)
I'm unable to become adult

A friend broke homeless
crashes on my bachelor couch
Misses a couple of nights

Whenever there's a news-
story of a man killing kids
and wife or maybe just the
kids. How could anyone do
that? Maybe I know

Who to kill in what order
me last for sure

Just the baby?
Let them live with that.
Kid and him?
Let her live with that
All of the above?
What the fuck why not?
then me

Brain becomes a hurricane in a chasm
blowing me away

A pistol in the neighbour's cottage, unlocked
just up the trail
fires me a message

When she, her new partner, toddler, come to see me
ask me to babysit
I throw a chisel at them
gouge the first growth fir floor

I live in a waterfront cabin down a forest path
Pacific Coast fir cedar hemlock alder ferns
Wood stove    mushrooms growing everywhere
I've a contact for pounds of pot
Tides washing in and out
A bay to swim in    across and back
Perfect hippie-in-nature wet dream life

Yet

I am sleepless destruction cycling in a cyclone
Damage seeking annihilation

I think I'll go for the really long swim
Let them all live with that

Waves wash through me
Water that feels like fire smoke and ashes
tides fall and rise
in a blue ocean
under a blue sky

colour of
absence

I'm still a baby crying
alone in a crib

a toddler being beaten
who knows he's alone

a teenage slave
under overseer affection

I am still
a tortured destroyed boy
going down down about to
chop down what little remains

of little me

No thing here makes me happy

Especially marriage    a yoke
Enough already with going through the motions
Never did want the white-picket-fence
Complete with a 30-year mortgage

"Sometimes," a biker friend says,
"We contemplate actions that if acted upon,
will ruin the rest of our lives."

Geese are flying south
In a V pattern    strong ones
take turns to lead

What happened to my pacifist idealism

Why am I stuck in the chasm bottom of a V
Why is my brain doing such violence to me
        I am not a has been
    Why am I so sad?    Marriage was a war.

Maple trees become red gold and brown
Alders and other conifers are bare
Days are shorter    time for me to shed some colour

            Wake up one morning

    Cut    shave off my beard and shoulder-length hair
        Sell everything I own    books    tools
                the whole shebang
    including table saw my former friend left with me

Love of wind and road beckons
Freedom    Again I'm alone
    finding centre of my cyclone

Will connect with my daughter later

I                              peaks
    flow with            and            of waves
            troughs                              swim with tides

    Hitchhike to San Francisco    LA
    San Diego Cabo San Lucas
    Hang out at Big Sur on the way
    Mexico City    Oaxaca

Puerto Escondido
Lake Atitlán Guatemala

A month later    tanned    short spiky hair
Don't recognize me in the mirror

Realize

No matter where I
go    there I am    all of me
and that's ok

Everybody is alive

# Stay and Save

James Boutin-Crawford

"Stay and Save," the large blue sign ran adjacent to Highway 99, right before the Oak Street bridge. *I might as well stay here in this cheap motel and save some money,* I thought to myself.

Cash was not a problem of late. It came free but with the cost of an ever-present feeling of impending doom. The sword of Damocles hanging by a thread just over my head. Only this banquet table seat was single and set for one, with fast food meals of loneliness.

Walking up to the front desk at noon, still feeling thick with the grog of rising from sleep, I pull out my wallet filled with my enemy's cash. A dot matrix printer noisily grinds away my receipt. The smell of ink, stale coffee, and laundry detergent registers, but just barely. A Ground Hog Day déjà vu feeling lulls me into a compliant patience.

A routine ID flash, the cash and change. "Thank you for choosing Stay and Save," is murmured from behind the reception desk. These rote lines, familiar and zombie-like, with tones of robotic subjugation.

*

Looking back, it is strange what is remembered and what is forgotten. I have no memory of the clerk's face. I do recall the emotions of sadness and dread mixing with dissociation and a fuzzy hangover. Yet even here, in this memory of a plastic melancholy, a light of the sanguine lives.

I was alive yet aimless. Knowing how to survive and knowing how to thrive are two different things.

*

Up the three flights of concrete stairs leading to the soda-pop vending machine, buzzing loudly, and back lit, night and day. A row of uniform windows and doors lead to my cell. Room #317. Opening a heavy-hinged door reveals a pastel-coloured décor of the late 80s. Bed, TV, desk, chair, bathroom. This shelter allowing a brief respite through meeting more than half of the day's hierarchy of needs. The polyester bed cover and starched sheets made for a not so comfortable rest.

Late nights spent with the company of the TV, filling time with talk shows and re-runs that eventually drift into infomercials, robust with pretentious forced energy, that soon promote channel surfing.

Click, televangelists' fervent declarations.
Click, payday loans advertising a low low rate.
Click, seduction offered in lingerie and a phone sex #.
Click, the soothing voice of Bob Ross creating happy little accidents that magically appear as trees growing upon mountains…..
Click, loud static with grey, black, and white snow.
Click, high pitched monotone signal and vertical rainbow-coloured columns.
Click, click, click …………

A garish lamp gets turned off at four a.m. The blackout blinds work, but neon red lights on the phone glow, and the digital clock shines brightly, keeping an angry vigil that breaks through the black.

*

Day and night blur into the same experience. Weeks turn into months. Only the weather differentiates one day from another.

The massive nude-coloured phone on the bedside table is decked with labels. From this glorious device, I will arrange times to meet others outside this hamster cage that I live in. "Save my soul" calls reach out after three p.m. to a pack of fair-weather friends, kindreds of a sort, brimming with teen spirit, whom I will gladly ply with free party favours in exchange for a momentary escape from boredom's reality.

I knew it was all a façade, but for the time-being survival and denial were coping strategies.

Where do I go?

What should I do?

"Survive."

All I can do with this guy, who was me, is put my arm around his shoulder and say, "It is going to be ok, buddy."

Chasing belonging with objects and subjects got old fast.

*

Bottles, beds, plastic and neon,
pizza, fast food, ash tray memories.
Bible in the drawer,
Cold beer and wine stores,
joints and LSD.
Petty crime,
trash can metaphors.

Surviving scores,
fist fights,
might is right,
entertainment and folly.
Strippers, hookers, and booze, playing the games that will cost ya!
Dignity.
Reality.
I could not see in front of me.
Fear's façade, a blinding log.
Selling or buying? Illusions.
Melancholy is a companion that is never too far away.

# *Saved from Suicide*

Kim Seary

lured back
from the dark ledge
at a roaring crosswalk

a slim girl with a deep red tuque
tucks her glossy hair into her coat
against the wind—that perfect pairing
of shimmering black
and ribbed woolly crimson
that fine-boned hand
so quick and pale

and then
eyes open
to furry magnolia buds
and here
a newly greening tree
lit brilliant from within

chest wide
almost forgotten
the morning curled in bed
against the world
the forced lonely walk
in the glare of sun
wind stinging
naked cheeks

# A Million Prayers

Kim Seary

She fell yesterday

tripped over her shoe-lace
in front of the library
two kind strangers behind her
lifted her up on her feet

It must have been their grasping
her soft under-arms

her heart thud out of her ribs
sweating    shaking
a crazy desire to hit out

no “thank-you”
could make its way
to her tongue

she is riddled with triggers
has worked—
not to let them go, that’s impossible—but to imagine new

neural pathways
forming like rivers
re-routed to feed fields of sunflowers
and lakes alive with fish

builds baffles
around her true Self
where the Holy untouchable resides

The thing is, she can't fight
can't march down Main Street
because in a hospital twenty years ago
she was locked-up
in a stainless steel room
stripped naked weeping for her child
for the gold cross her mother gave her

a room
with a toilet in the corner
a room
whose thick door would soon lock her in

a room
with metal bed—no blanket
a needle stabbed in her bottom
while five strangers look-on impassively
as if she were a dog
that had to be put down

but yes,
when she got out of hospital
she did not ask for help when she should have
for fear that her child
would be taken from her

and yes,
that has damaged her child
and taken precious years
to untangle
their mutual betrayal

and yes
it has taken years, a million prayers
and will take more years
more prayers
for her
for them
to be whole again

if ever

if ever

But what if
they are become new creatures
like beautifully bent trees
grown strong and green
their roots straddling giant nursing stumps
nurtured
by the sacrifice

# *Fairy Falls*

Kim Seary

In the midst of Saturday crowds in the market
where an artisan displays polymer gnomes.
I am alone, but flesh of my flesh,
you are always with me.

I think of the time we wore giant leaves on our heads
at Fairy Falls near your home in California.
You had to take my hand to help me go down under water,
and through a hole in a rock, where we stood screaming
under a frigid crystalline waterfall.

Your spirit has always been older than mine, my daughter.
I am so sorry. You've heard it a thousand times.
We all have terrible burdens to bear in this life.

Oh

How I wish we could stop wanting the other
to be other than who we are

Listen now

There are these bursts of magic and light
like at Fairy Falls with the giant leaves on our heads
transforming us to laughing water nymphs.
Perhaps we can meet there again, in that watery world
beneath the surface of things.

# *Born*

Kim Seary

Once my baby was born
I became really real
a real woman
with messes to clean up and fluids leaking
and sadness
so much sadness

I learned it was possible not to be loved
by a man—not to be cared for
and how suddenly this was of vital importance
all the other love had been just practice
But I hadn't practised enough or something
because now there was not-love
like an iron weight
a rusty foreign thing pressing down on my body
pressing and threatening

And on the other end
flowing out from love
love flowing from places I didn't know existed
flowing out and permeating
my fraught world like a rushing
river bursting its banks

My sliced-up womb ached and me cut in half
My ears buzzed
with exhaustion I'd never imagined a person could feel

I would watch my baby sleeping hover
around her study her round cheeks
her swollen lips watch her
breath move her little tweedle-dee body
in the sleeper my mother had bought

the dear round head
the blue eyelids
everything—
every single molecule of her a miracle

I would go into the next room for a few minutes
grab a piece of bread and slap
some peanut butter on it

put the kettle on the stove for tea

the whole time I'd be thinking of my mother
how my mother must have felt all
these things and then I'd cry
I cried and cried and cried
not bothering even to wipe the tears
How had I not known?
How could I behold this perfect
creature and ever hope to be her mother?

I can't carry the laundry basket
The salt water won't stop
pouring out of my face

I hear the baby stir
feel the twinge in my breasts
my milk letting down

the world shifts
and is filled in
every crevice
with that beautiful baby
I am filled with that baby
More filled with her than I was when she
was physically inside my body

I am aware and awake and flowing

I am bigger than myself and filled
with a faith like a train

There at the counter waiting for the kettle to boil
I close my eyes

The train's rhythm cradles us both

# *Ascension*

Kim Seary

In the desert of winters'
endless bed,
the stone slab of your death
presses on my chest.

*I want you back.*
I say out loud to the dust motes
and dirty dishes.

Your sister tells me
she feels you around.

I don't though.
I don't   and   I don't

through bleary springs
slog summers
and fog-stained autumns,
your absence permeates
like wet smoke.

But this spring,
occasional tree leaves
seem electric green
and
I've been snapping pictures
of garish flowers
and
singing in my car.

I think
I feel
my heart
growing back

Today is warm and blue
with fat scents
of sea-spiced lilac

and now you,
my darling,
are
everywhere

# The Price of Serenity

Kim Seary

You breathe and pray
down and down
deep and through
all the noise and layers
and images of yourself
that you worship

into a vast expanse
of oneness
where a distant memory resides

In the presence
of an unimaginable God
and without the benefit
of a burning bush,
there is something indescribable
somewhat like peace?
or tranquility?
or serenity?
something like that?
And then the next day

you go downtown to buy buttons
for your father's winter coat—
the one he pins his war medals on
every November 11

and you see a young girl
standing beneath a scaffolding.
She wears thin clothes
that barely cover her,
and an eye that is yellow—
a recovering bruise.

And you know
that she is yours now.
She is in you

She is you

And you are haunted
because you left her there.
you didn't even try
to take her home.

# Ordinary Salvation

Kim Seary

Holy One,
        Come and be in me

Like St. Teresa, pierce my heart
        with your arrow
        until my will spills out
        like wine from a broken bottle

Open my empty chest wide
        and fill me with You
        as I wash dishes
        and scrape away candle-wax

Let me be as nothing
        disappearing into Your Light
        as I sweep the floor
        as I call a friend lost in grief
        as I pay my tax

Smother my pride
with kisses and wiggles
from the small furry dog
that lives down the hall

Grow my patience
with the babbling cries
of a dear old woman
whose mind is lost

Open my eyes to see Your Glory
in serrated daisy greens
pushing up
from the black earth

Take me
and make me
forget myself

# Aetiology of a Depression

Ingrid Rose

The cloud of depression came for me when I was quite young. Not as the depression I've been forced to get to know for much of my seventy-four years. As a young person, I first witnessed it from the outside. Dad hiding under his bedclothes, unable to face the world. The words he could barely let out of his mouth as I opened my parents' bedroom door to say goodbye on my way to school. His trembled whisper, *Stay with me darling!* My instant reply, *Yes.* And I did.

Did I already know, then, this familiar feeling of being suffocated from inside? An inside I couldn't consciously engage with even though I'd pored over books way over my head. *Jane Eyre* at seven and three-quarters, as documented with my pencilled numbers on Ma's orange and cream paperback. Later on, but still too young for some of his grueling scenes in the mine, Zola's *Germinal.* Dostoevsky, Kafka, Anaïs Nin. I was fully at home with writers who plunged into their own troubled selves, swept along in the undertow, my anguish as acute as theirs. They encouraged me to empathize with Dad's condition. His vulnerability, blatant compared to Ma's apparent stability, had me firmly in his camp as soon as I began to engage with words. Likely even earlier. My antennae, picking up the currents of emotion swirling around in my family, particularly attuned to his.

From my first years at secondary school, on exam mornings, Dad would get me up early to walk off my terror, conferring on both me and my twin, Tim, our long relationship with walking. As both our parents worked, Dad's time to be with us alone was mostly relegated to Sunday mornings, allowing Ma to catch up on sleep and phone calls with friends. He'd walk with us through the parks in London.

Walking, as we learned early, and viscerally, keeps fear at bay.

Seventy plus years later, Tim and I continue this practice in Vancouver, thousands of miles from London, where our first steps on pavement were made.

In the 1950s, when we were growing up, the attitude toward, and understanding of, mental health problems was only just beginning to change. We were, perhaps, fortunate that Ma's formidable will to have our family appear normal meant that we regarded Dad's extreme depressions, as well as his highs, as a chemical imbalance. This was deemed less shameful, somehow, a flaw in his body instead of his mind. Body and mind were framed as peculiarly distinct from one another, though housed in the same skin. Dad's medical history, stitched together with story snippets, mostly from Ma, revealed that he'd first been diagnosed with nervous anxiety, at one point reframed as manic depression, which explained his behaviour and released him from the stigma of being considered crazy.

Not really crazy, like his youngest brother, Uncle Harry, diagnosed when we were seven or eight with megalomania, later to be termed schizophrenia.

Dad's family, the Roses, were clearly a source of concern.

Uncle Harry's condition began to betray itself in court. An articulate trade union lawyer, he'd demand high sums of compensation or nothing at all for a worker's injury in a factory.

As Harry's chutzpah spiralled out of control, the president of his men's club had Dad survey the stacks of mail written by Harry using their letterhead and sent to the "highest people in the land," the Queen and Prime Minister among them, and signed God. Dad, as the eldest son, was eventually required to commit him to a mental home. Uncle Phil, the middle brother, a bachelor who would have stayed in the army if he hadn't been turfed out for being vegetarian, got Harry released to live with him for the rest of their lives. In the same block of flats we did.

My uncles were viewed by Ma and her side of the family, the Buckmans, as really being the "mad" ones.

As much as she strived to protect us from Dad's condition, it couldn't be hidden from any of us living or working in our spacious flat in St John's Wood. Since both our parents worked as company directors, earning high salaries, we had a nanny who looked after us and Mrs. Reggentin, the cook, who came every weekday evening to make dinner. This privilege was fuel for my troubled political conscience, as was Dad's obsessive talk about politics and Marxism accompanying our Sunday walks, during which I was verbally responsive, while Tim would more often be kicking a stone like a football between his nimble feet.

Dad never hid the fact that he was a communist, as he was a born provocateur during any conversation with family, friends, and often, strangers. I was always proud of this and continued to have radical political leanings, that is until depression turned me inside out.

Surely Dad's bipolar disorder came in part from holding communist values and living as a capitalist. Uncle Harry's schizophrenia, too. To live with such tension without a part of one's self splitting off—improbable.

And then there was the feeling of shame that seeped into my being and became so pronounced during bouts of depression. Shame of the well-off and privileged home I came from. I'd been sent to a London County Council girls' grammar school, for free, whereas Tim, being a boy, had to go to an expensive "public" school, following in his Buckman cousins' footsteps. My closest school friends came from homes with less prestigious addresses and certainly no "staff." I always preferred visiting their houses, messy with life, family members, and lodgers everyone in the kitchen or living room together, rather than them visiting us in our quiet, pristine, tidy flat, confined to my bedroom. I tried hard to hide the fact we had a live-in nanny to look after us, a cook who came nightly to prepare dinner, and a chauffeur who drove Dad to his various places of work.

I never shared anything with them about Dad's "state." It announced itself by putting him into overdrive, words running into each other in his urgency to change people's minds until, with a sense of magnified proportion, he'd start to donate large sums of money to left-wing political causes. When fearless, he believed he could live with very little means. Ma did not. Her fear of impending financial ruin sucked all the air out of him. Guilt-ridden at having threatened the security she counted on, he hid away in bed.

In my family, our values and beliefs were not only lavishly conveyed through discussion and argument but also trumpeted by where we lived and our annual summer holidays to Mediterranean countries. To be quick-witted, vocal, and successful along with being the cleverest and most attractive went without saying. A trait, maybe, of our Ashkenazi Jewish heritage, apparent, at least, on both sides of our ancestry, although our paternal grandparents' stories were thin on the ground. If asked, Dad would flip the question, *Whaddya wanna know for?*

Not a single photograph of my father's mother, Rebecca Rose (née Pantuch, later Panto) nor father, Isaac Rose (née Rosenberg). Their change of name likely on arrival in London, from Warsaw, escaping the 1880s pogroms. From information gleaned on our walks, I know Isaac Rose worked as a tailor in the East End of London, read Hebrew, spoke Polish, Yiddish, and a heavily-accented English. A keen businessman who owned houses he rented out yet was ashamed of his inability to write or fluently speak his adopted tongue. He sent Dad and, no doubt, Phil and Harry to the Yeshiva, where they learned Hebrew and how to get answers by asking the right questions.

Questions upon questions.

Another gleaning. Dad's mother, Rebecca from a Russian-speaking family, also escaped the 1880s pogroms but, in her case, from Odessa, and ended up in London's East End, too. A shadowy understanding of Dad's family, left-wing intellectuals and cultured., I never knew them personally. Isaac Rose died when Dad was sixteen and Rebecca when we were toddlers.

Curious and confusing. Ma's parents were also named Isaac and Rebecca. Like Isaac and Rebecca of the Old Testament (which we didn't believe in). Isaac, the son who Abraham was prepared to sacrifice. But God stayed his hand. The end of human sacrifice—a huge step in terms of human history, it is claimed— but looking at the state of affairs today, I'd question if we ever really ended it there and to what extent that history still stains our DNA?

The Bible is one of those sources of human histories that are telling in terms of patterns that have deeply governed our psyche and actions. Even though we were not brought up to be religious or believe in God, I've wondered at the familiarity of events told in its many pages. In the Old Testament story, Isaac married Rebecca and begat twin sons, Esau and Jacob. Jacob came out second, like me. It is said he stole his brother's birthright. Sometimes I've pondered if I did that too, by being a father's daughter and engaging more deeply with Dad through discussion and argument than Tim, who was more expressive through his physicality than his intellect.

When Ma took us once a year on Yom Kippur to visit her mother, Grandma Buckman, in shule, and insisted my brother undergo his bar mitzvah—*For the sake of my mother!*—Dad swore he'd never be seen dead in a synagogue. Now, I wonder if he even came with us to Ma's older brother's home to celebrate the first night of seder. As children, we enjoyed the company of our Buckman cousins, especially the two closest to our age. Later to become highly successful in their respective fields of medicine and theatre, and die, both too young, from cancer.

That has often given me pause—both sides of their family, even more fiercely ambitious than ours.

The Buckmans, Ma's family, with seven siblings who all had offspring, primarily peopled our lives and, though never said out loud, surely were the ones we were supposed to take after.

Compared with this robust, physical, fun-loving, worldly lot, the Roses seemed to me to be as vulnerable and almost ethereal as their feminine name implied. As much as I often wished, especially at times of distress and depression, that I was more like Ma's line in temperament—grounded, earthy, and bold—I knew I'd inherited Dad's sensitivity along with his Marxist politics. Like his, my psyche was at risk. Dad would sometimes remark, his hand on my arm giving it a consoling squeeze, *You're a worrier like me!* The truth of it landing heavy on my chest. All those tears I cried when young, which Ma would try to curb by calling me, *Marie Pisher*, only making me piss them more abundantly.

It wasn't until I was twenty-one that I found myself in a state where I couldn't stop crying.

Depression had come for me full force at the end of my second year at university. It was then the scariest atmosphere I'd ever been in. A poisonous cloud coming out of nowhere and settling in my body. No wonder I feel uncomfortable writing this. More than uncomfortable. I keep having to get up and go into the kitchen in search of something sweet and chewy to settle me. My doubts trail along, *Have I gleaned any insights? Will writing about depression keep it from happening again? And again?*

At the time, it was recommended I take a year off. I was having what was then referred to as a "nervous breakdown." I couldn't look my friends in the eye. Unable to bear the shame of not living up to expectations that I'd get a first-class degree and follow it up with a glittering academic career. It felt like the end of the world. Who would I be now?

I wasn't entirely alone. Tim had failed his exams and been sent down from his university. Neither of my parents knew what to do when they found themselves with both of us back at home. Ma's best friend, Cis, recommended I see the psychoanalyst who'd helped her daughter during a sticky patch.

Psychoanalysis, an unknown quantity.

I hadn't read Freud.

The psychoanalyst I went to four days a week for the year I was living and working in London, and then when I was back at university, returning to London by train for a Friday evening and Saturday morning session, was a Freudian.

What I recall, fifty plus years on. Attic study in neo-Gothic Danish Church in Regent's Park. Old/young face seen only twice (no eye contact)—first and last visit. Glasses. Crumpled look. Brown suit. Dr. Brown. Depression has a way of obscuring colour. Everything murky. Hour upon hour on couch, eyes tracing lines on ceiling, branches of tree sweeping window, of stilted talk, of freezing as dry voice declares, *Now I am your Mother.*

Transference didn't work for me. Time did. Inch by inch, minute by minute, light began to penetrate murk, colour to return. Thoughts started to clarify, order themselves instead of trailing off into blankness. The crater that had opened up inside me and swallowed everything I knew and believed, along with my confidence, seemed suddenly to be filling in with a glint of interest. Interest in more than the food I'd been stuffing myself with, stifling painful emotions. Interest and feelings beginning to return. Depression's muteness transmuting. Sparks igniting purpose propelled me out of bleakness into a renewed sense of self. My authentic self, I assumed, but not so quick! Early days. Depression cocooned me. Coming out of it was a mixed blessing. Feelings. Relationships. Returning to that other reality where I had to prove my worth, become an adult.

Proving oneself. Becoming adult. It sometimes takes more than a lifetime.

Recently I've come off an antidepressant, escitalopram. I'd never taken an antidepressant before. Partly ashamed I couldn't manage on my own. Partly, because if the medication worked, what else could it do to my body? I took it for a year. It worked. The cloud that had seeped into every part of me, jumbling my thoughts, magnifying my fears and ineptitudes, dissolved. A calm soothed me. So much so, I could tune into the daily news, full of horrendous stories, and not be shaken to the core. This was a good thing, wasn't it? What I'd been trying to maintain for years through spiritual and somatic practices, not to be swayed this way and that by external circumstances. I still cared about the world and recognised my situation as privileged, but I'd come to see that if I wasn't centered, there was little I could offer my immediate circle and neighbourhood, let alone the larger one out there.

Depression still has its way with me. My dance with food, less fraught, but still there under the surface.

Uneasy relationships.

Regret—that I didn't ask the living about the dead as I begin to understand that ancestors anchor us. Not just to a place but also to deep time. Our place on the continuum. Now a deep somatic pull to the past. A search for forgiveness. Of myself. Of others.

Watering plants on my deck this early September evening, I notice a rose bush, overgrown by a peppermint plant, has put out new red shoots all up its thorny stem. They gleam bravely.

In an email of Sufi wisdom, a quote from Tagore, *When the string of the violin was being tuned it felt the pain of being stretched, but once it was tuned then it knew why it was stretched.*

Being stretched, I go to a number of somatic practitioners for support. When I tell my homeopath I'm depressed, she says she isn't scared by depression.

I still am.

# Letter to Caleb

Jessica Cole

The news still hasn't hit me. Today was pretty shitty to begin with, seasonal depression and all that. You know. I'm sure you do.

I'm writing this letter because I have no idea what else to do. It's been two hours since dad called, and I've spent every second of it sitting here in shock. The way he lifelessly said my name when I answered made it clear this wasn't a normal call. His long pause afterwards made me fear the worst: mom's cancer was back, Grandma Jill had passed away, Georgina lost the baby.

Then he told me.

Bad news has never been my thing. My emotions shut off and I step outside my body, my soul split in two. One half of me lives in reality, while the other half exists in survival mode. It's the latter that takes over when tragedy strikes. That's the version of me that said "okay" and hung up almost immediately. She's immune to despair—emotions are the responsibility of the other half. All she does is pilot forward, doing whatever it takes to survive.

It's the suddenness, I think. No part of me expected to hear you'd kill yourself, although lately you've been the last thing on my mind. I haven't seen you in years, haven't called you since at least two Christmases before COVID. Admitting this to dad or Georgina would break their hearts so I'll admit it here: talking to you was depressing as hell. Whenever we'd speak, you'd sink me so low that I'd take days to climb back to where I was before. I could only hear about your problems so much before I'd suffocate in anger over how little control you seemed to have over your own life. I could almost script our conversations in advance. Your house was a prison, you were sleeping fourteen hours a day and couldn't stop, the very idea of going for a walk felt like too much to handle. Early on, I learned there was no point offering advice you didn't want and wouldn't take. Maybe these calls were therapeutic for you, but they were absolutely draining for me. "Things will get better soon," you'd say at the end of each conversation. Yet here we are, years later, and they never did.

Part of me is guilty that the reason I'm not sad enough right now is because you were only my step-brother and not my biological one. I love you, of course, but not like I love Evelyn or Katie. We grew up together, without you. As much as it hurts to admit, you and I weren't very close. I don't know what your favourite song was, what you liked to do for fun, or how you met your wife. I'm not sure you even told me her name. The version of you I knew is from when I was six and you lived at home for a year, back when you would push me on the tire swing and sneak me scratch cards when dad wasn't looking. But I don't think you were that person for a long time.

Drinking constantly, your wife's restraining order, consistent unemployment. That's what I heard about you. Even though you didn't tell me about it, you told dad, and he could tell you were hurting. There's nothing I could have done, but that doesn't stop me from feeling responsible. Like if I'd stomached more of our phone calls, you might have told me before you did it. Maybe I could have talked you out of it. It's not true, but I still feel it all the same.

This letter, which you won't ever read and I hope no one else ever finds, is my way of saying I'm sorry, even though I don't have to be. You were my only brother and even though your life was yours to live, I still wish I could have been there for you. Hearing the news from dad made me want to call you, tell you that you're special and that I'm happy you're in my life. Now it's too late.

It wasn't selfish to kill yourself, even if dad feels differently. Hurt and unhappiness can be unbearable at a certain point. But that doesn't mean I don't hate you for it, for hurting us. You didn't even leave a note, and now that I'm writing all this down, I think that's what I'm most upset about. Not that you chose to leave but that you didn't say goodbye. No chance to convince you otherwise, no last conversations to remember you by. You're just gone.

What will your funeral be like? Would you have even wanted one? This is what I mean when I say we didn't know each other very well. I never told you that at my funeral, I want everyone to wear colours instead of black. It should be a celebration of a life lived rather than the mourning of one passed. There's no way dad or Georgina will allow anything like that at your funeral. They're not in the mood to celebrate, and to be honest, I'm not sure when they will be again.

I did offer to read a speech, if they want it. I hope you're okay with that. I figured dad isn't good with words, Georgina can't stand for that long, Evelyn will be too sad, and Katie might not even be there. If I could talk to you now, I'd tell you that I love you. That I'm sorry your life didn't end up being what you wanted, that you're a good person who had a lot of things get in their way and you made the best with what you were given. You didn't deserve the problems you faced.

But since I can't talk to you now and since the speech is more for us than it is for you, I think I'll tell a story. One of the strongest memories I have of you is the last time we saw each other, seven years ago at Grandpa's funeral. After the service, we drove to the city and hiked around Lighthouse Park. I'd wanted to do it because I saw it on Instagram, never mind that those photos were of a beautiful summer day and it was now late January, the sky grey and the air stinging cold. I didn't think you'd want to join. Even though it's an easy hike, I assumed a lifetime of smoking meant even the most basic physical activity would be too much for you to handle. But you surprised me, following me all the way to the rocks without a single complaint.

Did you know then that you'd kill yourself? Dad seems to think so. He says you've struggled with stuff for years, that he's shocked this didn't happen sooner. But to me, there weren't any signs of what was to come. You were your usual quiet self. Happy to be there.

There aren't any photos of us from that day. The view was more important to me, something I could post online to prove that I too had been there. I regret that now, the lack of physical evidence from our last adventure. All I have is a memory of you at the top of the cliff as the fog rolled in around us. Looking back at the path we'd taken. How you made it to the top all the same.

# Drying Out Uncle Romeo

Ronan Nanning-Watson

Damian and I are driving fast along the bumpy road to the Elaho out in Squamish Valley. My uncle Romeo is in the back and he's playing a song out of a Bluetooth speaker he brought with him. It's the song "Mandy's Discount" by this local band and it makes me picture an endless pit of impotent rage—I don't know how else to describe it. The lyrics are insane: *Since Mandy's at Alouette Correctional / For taking that cop's Heckler and Koch / Lying spread eagle on the sectional / I'm taking pictures of a perfect cock…* It is giving me a migraine and I'm starting to feel sick. Anyway, he's listening to that song on repeat as we're speeding along this bumpy road and I'm driving while Damian swivels back from the passenger seat to nod at Romeo. We go to this spot that Romeo likes. One that he's been to a bunch before.

"Realistically, they can all eat shit," Romeo says.

"Yeah," says Damian.

"Because you can trust the drug… You just can't trust the thug behind the drug."

"In what sense?"

"Drugs are not alive. They have no morality. They can't buy furniture—they can't choose what kind of cereal is good for the environment. It's not up to them what they turn people into. Do you know what I'm saying?"

"I'm not sure if I agree," says Damian.

My uncle is having a crisis. In the past he had what the family called "mental health issues" and "drinking problems," which alluded to a vague assembly of heavy drugs. Now he's allegedly "British Columbia sober," which means alcohol, weed, and prescribed ADHD meds. There is always a lot of bullshit going on in the blast radius around him but this time his wife Diane cheated on him with her boss. So he took a bunch of drugs, he won't say which, and now he's ready to kill somebody. Obviously we can't have that. Since he gets Ritalin prescribed it's likely he took a recreational quantity of that—that's probably where the teeth chattering sound is coming from, which I can somehow make out in a separate frequency amongst the pots and pans clattering on the washboard road.

"For example—don't interrupt me Rome," says Damian. "Listen—if you gave doctors acid *while they were operating*, they would do something stupid."

"No, not really," says Romeo. "Because, when you think about it, they would only be coming up by the time they were done the operation. Think about it." He shrugs.

Since I (more or less) recovered from my brain injury and talk a lot about healing, people with invisible pain seem naturally drawn to me. But really I'm drawing them to me. I can't tell if it's good or bad for me. Nobody else is going to do shit for Romeo. We've taken him out here while the family that he hasn't ostracized is trying to come up with a plan at home. His daughter, my cousin Quinn, got me to pick him up after work. We're basically trying to dry him out over the weekend so he'll come down from this state he's in and either go through a separation or work things out with Diane.

We go to this spot for a couple of reasons. One is that it's completely secluded. If he gets a hold of my keys to the car he could sneak back to the city, so we'll hide them under a rock. Then we can relax a little bit. Damian has brought some fishing stuff, which seems overly optimistic to me, but someone gave it to him so he wants to try it out. The second reason we brought him here is because my uncle is really into a lot of these alternative health and wellness therapies, and all the conspiracy theories that inevitably go with them. So anyway, one of the things he was really into in the past was the healing power of cold water. Romeo was fairly invested in it for a while, just sitting there like a can of beer in ice water. That interest was basically our only point of leverage in terms of getting him out of the city.

"We're going to the river," says Romeo, seemingly realizing it for the first time. I look back in the rearview and see fear climbing in his eyes. That's not good.

"It's pretty," says Damian.

I can see the river as we trundle past. The windows are fogged up but when you wipe them with a sleeve you can see the water carrying little bits of ice and snow downstream towards the city. It's cold enough that nobody else wants to camp. We're trying to get there before it gets dark, which is like 4:30. We're not seeing anybody else on this muddy forest service road, which is fitting because it feels like just by being here we're committing a crime. The song starts over again: *Five finger discount at Modern Harpies rack / Pre stained sweatsuit with dog whistle stamp / Slammed the herpes out of the girl in the back / Saying: "break me like an Ikea lamp."* The deal was that Romeo would go in the water. Where that gets complicated is now he's changed his mind, like I knew he would. His solution is to get very loud and become impossible to deal with. He doesn't seem to run out of energy, especially as a means of distraction. It's very overwhelming for me. It's not overwhelming for Damian who mostly thinks things like this are very funny, which is pretty annoying but also helpful.

"Remind me when we get there to show you this knot I learned. I learned it from this guy who reminds me of your uncle Jake… Oy! Can you hear me driver?"

"Yeah… Uncle Jake," I say. "You guys talk. I gotta focus on the road."

"You know what, maybe fuck the river, you know. I actually think the city is kind of the vibe right now. Practically speaking, this time of year, it goes against the grain, you know, of what our bodies are telling us—in the 1940s after World War II they found these French peasants who had been hibernating for ten years in a wine cellar. Circadian skipping…"

I put in earplugs, which I happen to have in my car, but I can still hear him trying to get my attention. Part of what makes this situation such a pain in the ass is that we had to take off with hardly any preparation. I left straight from work in my vehicle, which just so happened to have a bunch of gear in it because we've been doing a lot of camping. Damian just grabbed fishing rods, cigarettes, and an enormous puffy coat. We got some groceries on the way. Luckily I had the earplugs from doing target practice. So I finally shut the music and diatribes out.

I can tell from Damian's big ironic smile that Romeo is launching into a racist rant. It would surprise me if either of them believes any of it. It's hard for someone to really be accountable when they are in a state of surrender to internal catastrophe. Ultimately that's not an excuse: Romeo's been pulling this kind of shit since I was a kid. It is what it is. It's obvious to me, though, that he's trying to find something upsetting enough that will sour the mood so much we will turn around. I've seen this show a thousand times. The relentlessness feels like a means to an end: going back to town, more drugs, more escalation.

Damian points to a spot on the road and we pull up. I pop the trunk and just sort of sit there among the groceries on the carpeted cargo area of my CR-V, already exhausted. Romeo reaches past me to grab a jerry can of gas that he pours on a pack of firewood with the plastic still on and throws a match at it. The fire is huge. A whole night's worth of wood in one second.

Somehow it feels like everything he does, every tiny little movement he makes, is just to piss me off. I imagine hitting him in the face with the bag of potatoes. Damian finds everything he does entertaining. He's laughing in a way that is equal parts laughing-at and laughing-with, but Romeo is on his same page. Despite not being an artist or a patron, Romeo is quite involved in the art scene. Damian is an artist, so they cross paths quite a bit at parties and openings. They have their own relationship and that's part of why I asked him to come with. I knew I would end up as the parent at the birthday party.

I drag some more wood closer to the fire so we can chop it up later. They're walking to the water and I follow a few steps behind. We are surrounded by mountains. There's the river, which is pretty loud when you get close to it, but I still hear Romeo's mosquito noise. Since neither Damian or I are really responding, he seems to be shouting both parts of an argument, like he's forgetting he was the one who said what was so offensive or objectionable. He picks up a handful of mud from the ground to demonstrate something. I get the sense he took more of whatever he's on. Even through earplugs it is fucking insufferable. But my entire strategy is to dig in and outlast it. That's the whole project here. Three days maybe, then we drive back into cell service and see if we can come back. We don't have supplies for more than three days and I'm supposed to be back at work on Monday. I wouldn't be able to take him into town as is without him doing something unpredictable to create chaos.

Still, it's hard to watch. Damian is pretty relaxed, which I'm envious of. He finds racism hilarious. He's a Latino guy who has experienced a bunch of racism as well as being ostracized by both the white and Black communities in school. His response to it all has been that racism is fundamentally absurd and therefore funny.

Now Romeo has mud on his face and I think we're reaching the point in the speech where he goes across the anti-Semitic line of no return. I'm told that after you take a conspiracy far enough you inevitably arrive at anti-Semitic arguments. That's the vibe. The irony is that Romeo has a lot of Jewish family and history. His mother's father, my great grandpa, was Jewish. His parents were involved in the anti-Nazi resistance in the Netherlands. Many of our ancestors were interned or murdered in Auschwitz or Ravensbrück.

It doesn't bother Damian at all. He's said before that he finds chaos genuinely interesting. He's drawn to it. If someone's going beyond the pale, he wants to tag along. I can't hear Damian but he seems to be asking interesting questions because Romeo stops to think from time to time. This is a strategy I hadn't thought of. Damian always has an interesting perspective to consider.

While they're still talking, I walk around and find a long stick of driftwood, maybe ten feet long. Then I tell Romeo it's time to go in the water, and we start walking that way. But then he starts protesting, like he doesn't remember having agreed to go in, despite it being the whole point. His resistance is not ideal, because really it's the only plan I have. Without that I don't know how we're going to last. I'm not going to last, and I worry Damian will wind him up if I'm not there. Things will get out of hand. It's basically dark now, but you can see bits of snow coming down.

"Are you fucking crazy?" Romeo shouts while pointing at the river. "Look, there's icebergs."

Then begins this argument about him not getting in the water, but I'm not really listening, just marching forward with the stick. Initially I thought I'd put the stick by the shore so he could hold onto it, but I end up just driving him towards the water with it, like a lance.

"It's too cold!" he screams, slipping on the rocks and stepping through the ice.

"En garde," I say to myself.

This is the only hope I have to handle the situation, but there's also a part of me that would be satisfied just by making him uncomfortable. He's the one who used to do this cold water stuff, I tell myself. When I was a kid, he dragged me out to English Bay to do the Polar Bear Swim in the middle of winter.

He looks like he's going to cut across and Damian steps in to block him with his arms wide, like scaring a sheep into a paddock.

"I'm still wearing clothes!" he shouts. "Are you out of your fucking mind?"

"So take them off," I say.

"You're going to love it!" Damian says.

Romeo stands by the water with his heels on the ice. As he turns to look over his shoulder I shove him as gently as I can into the water and he crashes in. He lashes at the water, shrieking and looking for escape.

"One," I say. "Two…"

Neither of us can properly hear each other. He's up to his neck, holding onto the stick as it partially floats on the water. He's scrambling to get a hold on the slippery log, his hoodie floating flat on the water. He is drifting hard downstream in the current so I have to walk with the stick as he drifts, breaking the ice along the shore.

"Three… You have to go under water!" I say. "It doesn't count unless you're under water! Eight… Nine…"

"I *AM* UNDER WATER!"

"Eleven… You have to get your head under water…"

I see a stick going down the river past us. This river is bordering on unsafe. All of this is bordering on unsafe. Twenty.

He looks at me, eyes bloodshot. Thirty. Like suddenly locking eyes with a bear and wondering who is going to eat who. Then he goes under. Forty. With a dull look of terror he starts hauling himself in. Fifty. I let him. Sixty.

OK.

He runs over the rocks and starts tearing at his heavy wet clothes. Damian smokes by the fire, smiling in his Canada Goose jacket.

I hurry to the car to get a towel. I realize he's left that song going the whole time: *Since you're such a good friend / I'll give you everything / And everyone / But you let me down.* I click off the speaker with its stupid Bluetooth sound and take my earplugs out. It is so quiet you can hear the wind pushing the trees around.

When I get back to the fire with my spare clothes, I can see Damian in silhouette with a fishing line in the water. Romeo is staring into the fire with his arms around his knees, buck naked and pink like a suckling pig. The mud is gone and his face looks kind of like mine. We have the same cheekbones. He accepts the bundle of clothes from me without saying anything.

# the cost

Merle Ginsburg

born without a layer of skin. i have scarlet red skin. it glistens, it stings, it's raw, it's smoky.

fishnet. my skin is fishnet like the diamond shaped stockings. energy the colour black storms through me. it's not mine but it becomes mine.

it's a living furnace that doesn't have time to brew. it's on fire, ready to explode. there is impossible strength.

it's a plane slowly climbing to the forbidden zone. it has no compass, no boundaries. it shakes with power silently.

it's the grizzly bear facing me, his paws over my living room ledge. i look to the other ledge. he's waiting for me with long perfect menacing claws.

it's the tiny birds. their bodies are puffy, their feathers are sticky. their eyes are pin heads. their beaks are open because they can't breathe.

it's the rolling thunder in the distance. there's no lightning. it doesn't need an introduction. it's the rolling thunder in the distance coming for me.

# (em)bodying my story

Adishi Gupta

*what happens to the body*
*that,*
*with practice*
*perfects the art of*
*keeping it all in*
*clenching,*
*shrinking,*
*withdrawing,*
*with no place to go?*

We do not often talk about the body when we talk about mental health. Owing to the continued prevalence of Cartesian mind-body dualism, mental health is seen as separate from physical health, where the latter is met with significantly less stigma than the former.

Seven years ago, my journey navigating my mental health issues as a twenty-two-year-old started with a similar lack of awareness—I only wanted to stop my anxious and depressive thoughts, *quickly*. I had no idea then that my experiences of chronic health issues and feelings of detachment from my body were issues that could be addressed by psychotherapy.

As a queer woman growing up in New Delhi, I frequently experienced casual body shaming, like those so-called harmless, everyday remarks about my weight, skin tone, or body shape that people would pass off as jokes or "just being concerned." There was also the constant sexual harassment that came with simply existing in public spaces as a woman. Perhaps it was because of this that my body never felt like my own. Often, it was as if I didn't even have a body, that it was an afterthought, a burden. Even after more than three years of regular talk therapy sessions, I realized that talking through my traumatic experiences and emotions was not alleviating the overwhelming discomfort I experienced in and with my body.

I was not sure why I had such a difficult relationship with my body, but one thing I knew for certain was that other people's loving touch made me feel held and bodied. It is no surprise then that these difficulties were compounded during the extended periods of lockdown during the COVID-19 pandemic. Most days during the lockdown, I would lie curled up in bed, tightly clutching my touch-starved body, trying to trick it into believing that a loved one was holding me.

As the lockdowns eased up in 2021, I was due to move to Vancouver to pursue my master's degree at the University of British Columbia. Moving halfway across the world is a monumental event for anyone, but for someone with chronic health issues, such a move came with unique challenges. As I navigated my new life and learned to befriend unfamiliarity, I sought the help of mental health professionals with experience and expertise in body-based therapeutic practices. This was partly because my progress in talk therapy had plateaued after four years and partly due to the overwhelming literature on embodied trauma I had been exploring. As I became more receptive to understanding the body and mind as inseparable, I encountered the concept of a *bodymind*, a conceptualization proposed by disability studies scholars.

In 2022, I started seeing an Eye Movement Desensitization and Reprocessing (EMDR) specialist. EMDR is a type of psychotherapy that helps reduce symptoms of trauma. Using a combination of eye movements and guided instructions, traumatic memories are accessed and reprocessed to lessen the emotional charge and distress associated with them.

Though I had read a lot about how EMDR has helped people, I was still frightened to undergo it. Despite my fears, I was also looking forward to having an embodied sense of myself in the world, and of feeling more situated in my body.

My therapist spent several sessions establishing a trusting and secure relationship with me. Slowly, she introduced me to EMDR. She encouraged me to think of a distressing image or memory and describe it with as much detail as possible. Finding it difficult to conjure up a specific image or memory, I quickly questioned if I was in the right place. Gradually, I recalled a vision that I often see:

*I am curled up, trying to make myself as small as possible, a tiny ball in the corner of a pitch-dark room. I am trapped in the sickening and nauseating presence of the words "you are unlovable." It's not exactly as if someone is saying these words to me—it's more like they're just… there… heavy, suffocating.*

When I shared this vision with my therapist, she nodded gently, and we moved on to the next step of EMDR. I was worried about swift eye movements triggering my vertigo, so she asked me to start tapping rhythmically anywhere on my body with my eyes closed. Hesitantly, I started with slow, steady taps on my lap. She instructed me to notice the sensations, thoughts, and memories that came up while I was tapping.

*I feel the familiar nausea beginning to surface, rising with every tap.*

I was then cued to pick up the pace.

*The quicker I tap, the more it feels like I'm shaking something awake in me. Like I'm nudging my body out of the "freeze state" it's been stuck in for years. But it does not seem like my body wants to be unstuck. I think back to the numerous moments when I was so overwhelmed that my body just shut down as a way to cope. It is too used to this. So, it pushes back, resisting the unfamiliar, refusing to move.*

During EMDR sessions, my therapist would intermittently ask me to pause for a quick check-in. Most of the time I was not consciously aware of what was coming up. I could only tell that something was surfacing because I suddenly felt queasy.

However, during one session, I told my therapist about a painful and stressful experience with my parents that surfaced while I was tapping. She asked me to pause, take a deep breath, uncross my legs, put both my feet on the ground, and wiggle my toes gently on the ground beneath my feet. What followed was one of the most surreal experiences of my life as someone who otherwise struggles to visualize:

*My feet hit the ground, and something instantly shifts. I realize that while I was talking, I'd been this balloon just drifting around aimlessly, with nothing holding me steady. But suddenly, feeling the solid ground under me, it is as if someone is gently holding the string of the balloon. I am anchored in a way I have never experienced before. And in this moment, I feel... both held and grounded.*

Regardless of the kind of experience I had during each session, I was consistently dazed, confused, weepy, feverish, and achingly exhausted for days after every session. My therapist had given me a heads up that this might happen, but that still did not prepare me for when it did. It was distressing not only because I had never experienced this kind of sickness before, but also because I had no conscious awareness of what came up in that session. Not knowing was immensely unnerving.

Given how intense the reprocessing was, I can only imagine the intensity with which it had been weighing on my body. I talked at length about how disconcerting it was to become so viscerally aware that something I previously had no conscious awareness of had affected me so much. My therapist reminded me to trust my body's wisdom to protect me while reprocessing the painful memory and reassured me that my body's responses to the therapy were okay. She affirmed that they were a sign that the therapy was working and helping my body reprocess a lot of pain and trauma.

I walked into my therapist's office feeling like a stranger in my own body, but I left with a new sense of connection—a growing understanding of my bodymind. As I continue to navigate life in North America as a racialized, queer woman, I am learning to be more attuned to my bodymind and to tend to it in a world that rewards disembodiment. I am learning to be the gentle hand holding the string, preventing the balloon from drifting away.

*what happens to the body*
*that,*
*with practice*
*learns the art of*
*letting it all out*
*unclenching,*
*expanding,*
*reaching,*
*finding the space to grow?*

# Broken/unbroken sonnet

Neven Marelj

**Broken Sonnet**

I'll try to find imagery for you and I'll land on me,
covered in yellow paper, feet in stirrups, crying at the ceiling
my doctor is reminding me
that my body is remembering something I'm not.
but surely if my body is remembering,
that counts as me remembering, right?
I'll let words separate me from myself
I'll have given in to a choked verse
wherein my flesh becomes a thing
and my someone drifts away on a beam of greyblue light
remembering radiates through me
she examines my pelvis and i'm thankful
that my nerves can still tell my story
even if language can't make sense of it

## Unbroken Sonnet

i try to find imagery and I find me
feet in stirrups, crying at the ceiling.
my doctor reminds me that my body
is remembering something I am not
but surely if she has memory
that counts as my memory. *my memory.*
if i let the words separate us
then i will get caught in my own throat
wherein my flesh becomes another thing
and my someone drifts away on a beam
I feel her touch within our synapses
she examines our pelvis and I'm grateful
that nerves can excavate our stories
even if our mind can't lend us the language

# *Here's the room with everyone in it*

Neven Marelj

*after Ocean Vuong*

*Everlasting, can I call you that?*
if your skin betrays its shape
with each blinking day
the memory of swelling
shut feels the same

as if,

*as if*
*it's only when you try to forget,*
*the image stays clear*
the (accepting) brain
recycles less
leaves the tender walls of
the body to repent—

*remember*
*the most beautiful part*
*about you is your capacity to feel,*
the floor carpeted
with weeks
old laundry the boxes that remind you
you're only passing
by,

*in cups, everlasting,*

reminded
that life will always find
a new form
in cups,
the spores to dust
perspective from the lips,
the unceasing feeling of yourself collecting
in your bed,

*here is where you laid that love to rest*
here is a shallow pit,

*you can always*
*dig it up again*
a shovel to hit over its
head and a pen full of ink
for the dedication,

*below lies survival,*
*it took to us so well*
and yet, it never took to us at all.

# Coworkers, fragments, for Isla

Neven Marelj

your love built you a lamp        that looks like a house
cause you've always found trouble              in finding a home
lighting the way            our wrists to the purpling sky
pulling branches from fruitless fig trees
hope you'll learn to preserve                   this splendour
your co-worker comes by to teach us to can onion jam

pot bubbles slow slice slice caramelize save
skin to dye skivvies                  make ink to write
at the cutting board we work to not hurt
for babies that call us nanny or teacher
you've earned the name sister           from a child
who you imagine            is happier than you were

and we relish that kids don't shy away from onion
tears like we do              their brown saucer-eyed joy
at the movement of fluid and irritants        they teach us
the preservation of love is not of feeling but of practice

we practice

lamplit together at the end of your bed
we cook up a life where you and your dyke sibling
can raise dyke children        in a house where there is no yelling
as natural as the work the figs do to collect moss          we hold
each other
tight sealed through the winter

the rent increase is on the kitchen table
we're unmoved
          joyously
                    hungrily
                              clawing into the dirt in the yard
                              they can't steal the land from beneath
                        my acrylics
I wash up after, and
when you witness me naked between the bathroom

and my bedroom I am unafraid

cause I know you would rub lotion on my body
if I my hands gave way            will light the entry
when I get home late      will keep my lid on
when I lose the weights            you know
                                          always
                                                I will do the same

# Summer Apocalypse

Danica Longair

2018. August. Saturday.

The amber light shrouded them in bed, the blood sun low in the smoke-choked sky. The forest fires raged in not-too-far-away lands, nature's warranted tantrum against human indifference. Reed hadn't let Jane go since they brought her home Friday evening. All the pair could do was collapse into each other's arms. It had been quiet all day. Their cats curled into spirals at their feet on the faded and stained coverless comforter. Only two more nights until Jane had to go back.

Reed was grateful to have her home, but their muscles were stiffening from being locked around Jane. They must keep her safe. Protect her. She didn't seem to want to move. They wanted to get outside, see the world beyond the haze. It would be good for Jane, for them. But Jane was concrete under covers.

"We should do something tomorrow." Reed extended a hand toward Jane's temple, pulled it back. "Sunday Funday?"

Jane didn't move, her gaze firmly set on the bare wall, her brown eyes dazed. Then, in monotone, "Sure." Then, "Okay."

"Beach day?" Reed offered, then cringed. Dark waters, a depth unimaginable, voices screaming against the wind and waves.

"No. Thanks," Jane said, turning her head further. "The air. Your lungs."

Reed's lips quivered upward. Jane was considering Reed's needs, their asthma.

"What about Granville Island? The market is indoors. We haven't been to Oyama in months. Let's finally get a slice of Ibérico ham." Reed salivated. Jane rigid in Reed's arms, her head cold against their chest.

*Buzzzzz*

Reed could hear their phone from the living room but turned their head the other way. They had all they needed.

*

Leave. This. Bed.

No.

Jane's stomach tightened and burned.

No.

Cocooned: wrapped in comforter and strong, gentle arms. Buried in cement. Can't move. Don't *want* to. Safe.

Here. With Reed. Safe.

Home. Cats. Privacy. Safe.

Safe for two more nights.

*

"Sunday," Jane said. "Too many people."

The tabby cat stretched her body from snail to snake, ending as a sphinx.

"TV?" Reed asked.

The TV was in the living room of their rented apartment on Main Street. They'd have to at least get out of bed, which Reed felt would be best for Jane.

*Buzzzzzz*

Reed wondered if the ignored calls were from Lillian Kato, their boss, who raised an eyebrow over Reed's need for time off from the restaurant but always relented. She had opened the Gastown hot spot the previous year, her first as executive chef. Reed had rushed home to tell Jane they got the fish chef job under Lillian, only to find Jane curled up in bed. Their shoulders fell like a cleaver to a salmon's head.

Now, with so much work missed, Reed should take a shift. This is the dream job. But Jane is the dream girl. So fragile, as though the wrong word would shatter her, a hammer to a Venetian vase. Millions of pieces Reed would have to glue together alone.

There was only Reed, since both of their families turned their backs on their "choices." Queerness, in all its complexity, got a simple response—no, out, ghosted. Reed was unsurprised by their white, small-town-religious parents' reaction. Still, devastated.

Reed had called Jane's mother, Mrs. Zhou, about the involuntary hospitalization.

"It's your fault she's there," Mrs. Zhou said. "Your fault she's this way. Your fault I can't see her, hold her, love her." That was weeks ago—Reed assumed Jane had not heard from her family.

Jane looked towards the semi-blinded window, which painted bars of lifeless light over her. "What time is it?"

"Almost five." Their eyes widened. They hadn't eaten all day. Weren't they supposed to feed Jane? Solid meals were a part of recovery.

"You hungry?"

"I could eat."

Reed hid a smile. Jane had lost so much weight.

"DoorDash from Hachibei? If we order now, they might still have some black cod."

"Okay." Receptive. Hopeful. Black cod saikyo yaki was her favourite.

Reed found their phone and tapped the screen.

*Buzzzzzzzzz*

*

The smell.

Fish.

Another food tray.

Reed, sitting at the foot of the bed, chopsticks back and forth to their mouth.

Reed stops, food dangling.

Fish dangling.

Fish under her.

Deep. Down. Dark under her.

Fish would nibble her, eyes and skin, muscle and organ.

Fish devour brain cells.

*

"It tastes good," Reed said.

She's not eating. She's just sitting there, turned towards the bathroom door. Reed thought the fish would be gobbled. Fish was brain food, too. Jane hadn't even unwrapped her chopsticks. The pale bamboo rectangle sat peeking out from the white and green sleeve, unbroken. Reed couldn't force her to eat.

The light bled through the leaves of Jane's dried-up ficus.

*

Sunday

Reed snored beside Jane.

Jane wasn't supposed to check Twitter.

Phone in hand. Feed on screen.

*"The US president's tweets are absolutely insane. Like, straitjacket insane." - @Wokegirl88*

Jane stifled a gag.

People assume evil is crazy. Crazy is evil.

Requiring straitjacket.

Electroconvulsive therapy.

Drugs to save the world from crazy evil.

Jane balled her fists.

Knees to chest.

*

Reed's cruel dream was still lapping at their consciousness—swirling dark water and blood-infused air—when they awoke and squinted out the window. The same smoky sky.

"Morning." Reed didn't go in for a kiss like normal, worried about giving Jane space. Jane's eyes dropped. Reed doubted themselves.

What was that stench? Reed glanced at the dresser and saw the red-and-black plastic takeout bento boxes, the tuxedo cat's head inside one, snacking.

"I should feed the cats," Reed said, rolling out of bed and pulling on a pair of jeans. They paused and turned back to Jane. "You okay?"

Jane nodded. Reed sped to the front door and splashed a scoop of food across the cats' bowls, noticed their water needed to be changed, then glided on socked feet back into the bedroom.

Jane coughed, elbow to mouth, revealing her reddened, slashed wrist under hospital bracelets. Her eyelids wrinkled.

Reed wondered how they would explain all of the scars to their kids one day. Could they bundle it with a conversation about mythical blue skies and orcas for a discussion of all the horrific losses in the hypothetical lives of children yet to be?

*Buzzzzzzzzzzzzzzzzz*

*

What day was it?

Jane turned her head towards a wall calendar. Granite encasement feeling… lighter?

Sunday.

One more night.

Why was the sky like that? Yellow. Thick. Suffocating.

Burning smell. Did Reed make toast?

Should they be getting ready for work?

Reed loves that job.

*You are not responsible*, the therapist's voice echoes.

*All your fault*: Jane's thoughts.

Jane pulled the sheet up to her collarbone. Rolled away from Reed.

*

"So, how about that TV binge? *Nanette*, finally?" Reed said to Jane's back, her body facing the bathroom door. They should have removed the triggers in there. Jane probably didn't want to go in. Her bladder must be bursting. But with what? Was she drinking any water beyond the sips with pills? So many pills…

"I watched it last week. Sorry." Jane's voice a whisper in a tunnel.

Reed's lips drooped. "What about that new teen romcom that everyone's talking about on Twitter?" Reed cringed. Jane wasn't supposed to be on Twitter. How could she know about it?

"Watched it, too."

Still no movement. At least she was doing something on the ward, using her iPad, not just staring into space like some others, who terrified Reed. Jane had been one of them—did she know that?—in those first days of hospital gowns and little else. Why did the staff there have to drug people into oblivion? There must be other ways to save a life.

"Well, what do you want to watch?" Reed asked Jane's back.

"I don't know."

Reed felt the churning in their stomach suddenly harden. How much longer would she be like this? Weren't the meds supposed to be ending this? Reed remembered they were supposed to be grateful Jane was alive, but would she ever be *alive*, and also, *herself*?

Jane turned her whole body, slowly, to face Reed. "What about that show with Amy Poehler and whatshisname? The one about crafts?"

And there it was. The glimmer, ever brief, of the woman Reed loved, whose smile brightened something in them, who loved her city and food and pop culture with such passion, who would obsess about a new TV character for months, who could show interest and care for things.

"Oh, yeah! Let me Google it," Reed looked at Jane for that glimmer, but it was already gone. Maybe it could come back. They grabbed their phone from the bedside table and, after another lingering look at their love, turned to the screen, swiping up to avoid their messages.

*

Jane turned her head back to the bathroom door, grateful it was closed. Her mind meandered back to water, could feel her chest rising and tightening with the undulating waves. She shook her head once and reminded herself to breathe.

Reminded herself she was safe, here, with Reed.

Comforter cocoon.

No razors. No water. No darkness beckoning.

Fog, haze, a blanket. Safe.

One more night.

*

Reed couldn't find the craft show on Netflix.

"Don't worry, I'll find it," Reed's voice panicked that they wouldn't find it streaming.

They did.

They stayed in bed, watching the show on a network website with Reed's laptop. When the credits rolled after the losing contestant tearfully hugged the other crafters, Jane turned to Reed. Briefly, Jane made eye contact. The motion relaxed all the stiffened muscles in Reed's body. A thread between their bodies weaving itself back together. But then, her eyes closed and… the moment… gone.

Reed watched Jane's breathing, grateful for the expansion and deflation of her chest. Sweat was starting to mix with the fish smell. Showering, leaving Jane for that long, was too scary. Jane should shower too, but with razors and pills gone. Jane's hair was greasy and sticking to itself. It normally shimmered in the light, the indigo streaks long faded.

"I guess I have to go back… *there*," Jane said, pressing her eyes closed.

There.

The paramedics had ferried Jane there—the hospital—that night, having pulled her gently down from the bridge's pale green railing, so high above a black watery death. Jane was desperate to finish, her wrists still bleeding from her failed attempt. Local Twitter a firestorm of petty people complaining about the "police incident" on the Cambie Bridge blocking traffic to the English Bay fireworks show.

*"Just effing jump" - @YogaislifeVan*

Police later said she must have wandered to the bridge from home, leaving salty blood drops along her meandering path. If only Reed hadn't worked that night. But the fireworks customers meant all hands were on deck.

Jane had seemed okay earlier that day, at least on Messenger with Reed, using more than one word to answer.

When they got home, the apartment was empty but for the blood.

Reed's hand shook as they pulled the phone out of their jeans pocket, tapped 9-1-1.

It was happening again.

Where was she this time? Would they use the restraints again? How long until she'd get a weekend pass and be home again?

"Reed?"

Reed was jolted back to the woman—here, now—in their bed, safe. August smoke suffocated the city.

"Not until the morning," Reed responded to Jane's lament, tightening their grip on Jane's hand.

"Reed?" Jane's face turned towards them. Reed felt like they were looking at each other for the first time in months. Jane had umber craters under her eyes. Her cheekbones were sculpted, her cheeks sunken. But now, there was the slightest spark of fire in her irises.

"Yes, love?" Reed replied, their lips and chest rising.

"I don't want to go back there again. I mean, after they let me go, I don't want to be hospitalized again. I want to get better." Jane sat up. "Do you think I will?"

Reed took a deep breath.

Over a decade had passed since Reed was scrubbing dishes and Jane was counting her tips into coin rolls. Reed thought Jane's long, messy, purple hair tied back for work was luminescent. So, they made her a little something to eat one night when their old boss wasn't looking: seared scallops with a brown butter sauce and a pinch of fresh thyme. Jane did not last as wait staff. Reed learned to take the days one at a time, to stop thinking of logistics and revel in future fantasies like a glowing, pregnant Jane.

So why did Reed love a woman who didn't want to live? Who wanted to die, knowing Reed loved her, knowing it would ruin Reed?

Reed indeed hated the deep, dark waves of bedridden Jane, but they loved when that spark in Jane's eyes took over her whole body. Why else would they be together if not for a belief in happy tomorrows?

"Of course," Reed replied and felt the certainty of it in their bones. It's all they needed.

Hope.

That's how you stay alive.

*Buzzzzzzzzzzzzzzzzzzzzzzzzzz*

Reed lingered in Jane's gaze while reaching for the damned phone. They looked down just long enough to type, *"Sorry, Lillian, I won't be coming back to work. I resign."*

"I just quit my job," Reed said with a smile.

"Wait, what? You quit? But you've worked so hard for that job!"

Jane's monotone was gone, replaced with shock, her eyes wide, not deadened. Reed's smile broadened. They did not know how they were going to pay the rent, or keep up their Hachibei habit, but they knew one thing for sure: Jane would get better one day, and they wanted to be there to see it happen.

In the morning, Reed would drive Jane back to the hospital, her weekend pass from the psychiatric ward expired. They had this one more night together.

*

Screensaver on laptop—bursts of light fading into dark.

Cats curled into one another, settling into each other's softness, closing eyes.

The stench of yesterday's black cod absorbing into the fabric of the duvet.

A siren rising and falling.

It rages through traffic towards

someone else.

# 7 lbs. 6 oz

Lenore Rowntree & Beth Rowntree

Some things about my sister Beth
that I can't think about for too long
without getting sad and confused:

1. The time we went to the Bracebridge
Dairy for cherry pie and vanilla ice
cream and she took too long in the
bathroom, so I kept knocking on the
door, and when she emerged she said,
"My life is hard, you know."

2. The time I blew snot out my nose
and rubbed it in her hair in front of
the boys from down the way who
were already afraid of her.

3. The time my aunt said at the family
reunion that she ruined everything.

4. The time kids threw snowballs
at us on the way home from school,

and only the ones they threw at her
had stones in them.

5. The time a man gave her an engagement ring that was too big for her
finger so it came off during the night
in her bed, and the staff at the group
home found and returned it to the
man, who'd spent his disability
allowance on it, and she thought he
had broken up with her because she
lost the ring, and nobody ever told
her anything different.

6. The time I looked in her purse and
found nothing but scraps of paper so
covered in writing there was hardly
any white left on the pages.

7. The time my mother told me she had
a normal birth weight, 7lbs. 6 oz.,
but an abnormal delivery because a
bully nurse shoved her back in and
held her until the doctor arrived.

8. The first time she became an
outpatient at the Clarke Institute of
Psychiatry and wrote this list to
remember the layout:

11th floor
Dr. Jeffries' Office
9th floor
8th floor

7th floor
6th floor
5th floor
4th floor
3rd floor
Day Care Centre
Ground Floor
Chapel

9. The time I found her poem "Lies" in
her wastebasket:

Happy
Jolly
Jovial
Pretty
Funny
Beautiful
Cheerful, Pleasant
Lovely, Sense of Humour
Educated, Famous, Smiling
Lies, Full of Lies, A Wheat Sheaf Full of Lies.

Notes About Poem: Two sisters—the similarities are many, the differences few. The poem explores the subtle things that determine who gets a gentle ride in life and who gets a rough one. Many aspects of the poem are found. Emotions found in Lenore's memory, triggered by poems found in Beth's wastebasket, purse, desk, and dresser drawers. Lenore tries to write every day and often fails. If Beth had her way, she would never stop writing.

# *How I Cope*

Beth Rowntree

I cope with schizophrenia
by taking medicines and medications
by being my own best friend
by eating cherry pie

miracles needed in my mind and body! etc!!
genie lamp needed in my mind and body! etc!!
sounds of silence needed in my mind and body! etc!!

peace amongst the worlds
no warful sides
only truths and truces

*you'll feel better in the morning in your schizophrenic shoes*

I cope with autism
by looking people in the eye like a contented Siamese cat
by people who have autism being honest about their
temper and anger

by people who don't have autism being honest about
their temper and anger

*ye sow, so shall ye reap*

# *Her Brain*

Lenore Rowntree

Her brain is a Swiss cheese
a dehydrated, Swiss cheese
a dehydrated, Swiss cheese on drugs—she is
the Woman in the Moon
seeking gold
specific gravity 19.3.

A fistful of meds, Ativan *prn*,
and she is beyond

heavy

she is smeared

so far out
the black holes in her mapping fray—still,
her brain circles the Heavens
defying g
r
a
v
i y.
t

# Silver Remains

Amy Wang

### I.

Everything began as silver and tarnished to green of hospital uniform.

### II.

Prior to my hospital stay, I hardly slept. Nights were spent procrastinating until my mind spun. My room was cramped and yet I was never still within it. The tiny kitchen trashed with countless plates; mess-filled couch with overflowing shelf opposite. I collected books I couldn't read. My concentration was shot. Every night I scrolled the web until my senses fled. Whatever sunk its claws into my head,

each day it pulled ever so gently until

my psyche slipped off.

I dragged myself to the nearest emergency in hopes that someone could sew it back on. Between broken bones and nocturnal fevers, someone said, "Not really sick, are we?" It could've been that thing with the claws. But everything here had the potential to hurt. Every so often I bent over in my seat, sick of myself and the people around me.

Soon, triage: this nurse wore a sky-blue uniform. Her nails clicked against the keyboard. A silver bracelet dangled from a wrist with charms that winked at me. She gave me a bracelet to wear. This one made of blue paper.

### III.

Consider what it means to stand before locked doors. Nicked wooden handles wrapped in silver chains. Who would break into a place like this? Most times we were imprisoned with the doors wide

open.

### IV.

I shared a room with two other bodies. One arrived days after me. The one before, Lily, screamed when the nurse opened the door at midnight for my arrival. In the morning, she said, "It's nothing personal, I thought you were a ghost."

She later stole my silver-spined book gifted by a friend and

this I did not forget.

### V.

The ward had been folded into another hospital. But I'd come to see what was left behind. I pressed my ear against the door, heard nothing but a hum

that radiated

through

the wood.

It traveled through my cochlea, into the fluid my brain steeped in, and along neurons as wires. Soon it found circuitry left by doctors who treated me: bright silver sparks where memory shorted.

## VI.

"Sleep is very important," said my psychiatrist. Our daily interviews took place in the glass-walled room. Fluorescent light glazed his leather shoes. He tapped against a clipboard he brought everywhere. People walked by. They watched our lips move, but no sound ever reached them.

"I can't sleep," I said.

"We'd better fix that, or else your health will slip through your fingers like quicksilver."

Quicksilver is mercury. In Chinese, mercury is *watersilver.* Thought to be the elixir of life, it killed one emperor searching for ways to live forever. It was once the cause of madness in the West.

## VII.

The hum was not enough to replicate construction workers pulling up worn carpet, flipping over old couches, stacking plastic chair upon chair—the day this place moved on without me. I longed to witness the physicality of

deconstruction.

I wanted to know who finally shut the doors. I wanted to know who owned those silver chains.

## VIII.

Some therapies resembled the madness they hoped to cure. On the day everyone received electroconvulsive therapy, they skipped over me.

"We'll increase your medication," said the psychiatrist when I asked. "You don't need ECT."

Fellow patients and friends fasted for the day. A row of chairs ran along the back wall of the dayroom. Swaddled in blankets or clothed in shades of mint or beige, they waited their turn for electricity. I imagined silver electrodes clipped into wires of brain.

"It doesn't hurt, I've had it done dozens of times," Lily said. She had my book in her hand. Memory loss is a side effect of ECT, and she'd forgotten who owned the book. Soon,

she would forget me.

After the treatment, my friends would sleep. Long, deep sleep that passed through doors when I walked by their rooms. This sleep must've smoothed over fissures in psyche. But this sleep also terrified me with its ability to choose memories at random. The most precious ones it would keep, and with return there was no guarantee.

Later, I began to lose memories. By then I'd already left the hospital.

"You'll be safe," the nurses once said. They didn't say my medication was twice the legal dosage. I only knew safety in handfuls of pills, stones along a pathway. I walked upon every pill that granted me sleep. I lost myself with every step.

### IX.

The door was cool upon my forehead. I sensed the hum against my skull that seeped into my brain. I wanted to take something. I knew there must be rubble, fragments of myself. I pulled at the handles. I placed my hands onto the chains. I waited for my brain's circuitry to rewire, for the silver to return and

tarnish to escape.

# On Embodied Memories

Amy Wang

We remember some things, forget the rest, and these compose our memories. What about memory beyond the mind and image—have you considered it?

Visuals change when we recall memory. Your trust disappears with each iteration. And I will be honest: I do not trust the mind that holds my memories any longer.

The mind is prone to change. It is fragile. There exists a layer of dura mater, but no membrane or skull can protect this brain from an assault on the psyche. In April of 2018, I was hospitalized and

> this lasted for one month which is plenty of time
> for experience                                   (injury)—

I was not given a high dose of medication at the beginning. It was gradual. I met doctors in small rooms akin to interrogation. Soon I rose beyond the legal dose, a crime only acceptable because it took place within the institution. Side effects followed. I dropped all medication once I left the hospital, and this withdrawal shattered my mind. Such debilitating pain drove me back to medication. Then away again. Constant pharmaceutical push-pull with my cognition / psyche / remembering

destroyed three times.

Those memories, those visual thoughts, they're now incomplete. Little things are left. There are fragments to pick over: colour of hospital clothes, mealtimes, people I spoke to. But everything I supposedly lost is still here, as

every forgotten prick of needle,
glass-walled room, medicated dream,
is replicated by feeling.

My memories were still extant; they'd noticed the psyche's deterioration and fled. Not sold nor stolen but alive: repurposed into body memory, known through the body. Here they found home. What brain matter once held was now deeply embedded in bone and tissue. I could no longer see them, but they did not need to be seen to exist.

In the hospital I existed in a state;
this state now exists through sensation.

I never left the hospital nor had it left me.

These hospital memories still resurface when necessary. When I'm on the verge of bad decisions, the trauma returns, folding along my spine, taking root as tension. It grows hostile in my arms, shoulders, chest, and I must pay attention—

I did many things after hospitalization that always embarrasses my entire being. I never understood the deep-rooted shame / repulsive anger / the parts of me that took issue. But now I know them as memories in my body; ones who'd been trying to tell me not to make those decisions. But I hadn't listened,

nor any recognition.

I still cannot trust my mind. I cannot blame it for being victim to the weapon of pathologization. But trust has disappeared and rehomed itself into the somatic, with safety in unfragmented body. I can trust how my skin tightens at a certain decision, how bones ache, how palms prick before perspiration. I can the trust within my body and remember

these embodied memories.

# *kōng shǒu (empty-handed)*

Amy Wang

**I.**

mama, i am looking for you in these
pages and communities. places that might
hold you

in records and recollections
of our culture when you're gone.

but these pages have no traces of village
you came from, nor glimpses of hebei

only unknown traditions
in languages unspoken.

locating you:

history full of laborers, railroad
workers, gold miners, cantonese
immigration—

but mama,

when you arrived from *your*
north, more familiar with flour
than rice, countryside than
curbside—

it was long after the head tax was gone.

**II.**

mama, i am looking for you in these
words and thoughts. actions that might
hold you

in respect and resurrection
of your being when you're gone.

but these sentences never reflect the girl
you were, nor the education

unknown to family until *you*
graduated first.

finding you:

history full of male calligraphers,
scholars, social classes above
rural farmers—

but mama,

when you opened books in *your*
countryside, picked up pencil
and learned to read and write—

it was what led to you and i.

# suppose

Amy Wang

you never expected to be a mother. and you didn't approach anything with the expectation (to remember).

you were carefree. you wanted to read. your hands roamed dusty village shelves and corners. technical manuals, newspaper scraps, scribbled napkins as literature—

> family / friends / relatives who never under stood the written material.

you read from sun-up to sun-set. and suppose there was never an expectation to go further with the text. you only wanted to know stories beyond your own

> and they hardly seemed more than simple (brilliant) existence.

you had no expectations for this knowledge. nor where it could exist.

and how many times

have i wanted to travel in time to find you in the dark,

reading beneath the porcelain moon?

how many times have i wanted to travel, just to know

you before you?

# *instructions*

Amy Wang

they want their mothers dead. they speak of mothers as leopards; sleek and discomforting. they want their mothers gone. this includes mine. i cannot tell them i love my mother. my mother is supposed to be in books, movies, and conversations around tigers. my mother should be spiteful. she must be bitter. she must be traumatized. they will assign her the trauma if she does not cooperate. i cannot tell them she grew up between grain and love. my mother should have existed in oppressive cities beneath oppressive family histories. her upbringing in wheat fields is an anomaly: scrub it clean from her and me. they want the abuse normalized. it will be repackaged as commercial confession, the eternal memoir. their mothers cannot love so i cannot say how our calls end with beautiful confessions. we are here to be endless duplicates of agony, all leftovers deposited into the sinkhole of this exploited earth. my mother is supposedly a generous wound. if this is pain then why does she hold me. my mother tells stories they don't believe. she must be sanitized for them to digest. i cannot tell them she never hurts me. i must smile when entering communities bonded over cruel maternity; mothers who are intolerable, mothers who never smile with affection nor say so. her history in poverty is why they want her to destroy me. they want pain to be ours. i cannot tell them my mother loves me. my mother isn't supposed to exist.

# Shelter

Kate Bird

Icy shards of rain stream from my umbrella and seep up the sleeves of my raincoat as I race to a work Christmas party at the Hotel Vancouver. Neon signs and Christmas lights along Granville Street blur into soft focus slicks of colour and sidewalks glisten fools-gold under streetlights. Only a few cars slide past, dark against dark. Rainwater gushes down the gutter, pools at the storm drain. So much rain.

A woman appears before me. I stop. Peer up from under my umbrella. Pale gaunt face, dark circles, rain-soaked straggly hair plastered to her forehead. She shivers, clutches closed the thin fabric of her coat. Her quiet voice, thick and toneless, asks—do you have a dollar? She extends her cupped hands, collects raindrops as she waits, then lowers them. They hang limp at her sides. There's something about her shadowed eyes, her quivering voice, that flusters me. I shake my head, mutter no, rush past her up the street.

*

My father didn't set out to become a drunk. Neither did my mother. It was an incremental process, an accumulation, over time, of life events and personality flaws and societal influences of the 1960s.

I was ten when my mother's beloved father—the person she felt loved her most and understood her best—died suddenly of a heart attack. His loss plunged her into devastating grief. Looking back, I now understand how fragile and depressed she was in the months following his death, but at the time I found the profound shift in her frightening. She vibrated with nervous anxiety, and I often woke at night to the sound of her weeping.

I watched her anxiously, closely, constantly. I watched her deeper than just the look on her face and the tone of her voice. I watched her soul. Mom's mother also kept an eye on her. "Your grandmother had your mother under constant surveillance," an aunt once told me. "She counted your Mom's drinks and commented on their number and frequency." The weight of her mother's and daughter's hypervigilant gaze must have been unbearable. And so Mom drank secretly. And more. Each evening she'd open the door of the dining room cabinet and pour another glass of cheap wine from the gallon bottle she kept there. Quiet as she tried to be, the click of that cabinet door latch could break through any distraction I tried to put in its way.

My father drank alone in the basement. Later I learned that he was under terrible strain at work, and that deep insecurities about his lack of education undermined his self-confidence. He rarely slurred his words or acted drunk. It was the way his little finger stuck out from his hand that warned me to stay away. Because sweet and loving as my father often was, he could turn crude and dangerous, his booming voice yelling at me to get the hell up the goddamn stairs before he kicked me in the slats.

A year after my grandfather died, my mother returned to full-time work, and my parents suddenly had the money to drink. And drink they did. Drinking was the rip current that dragged them into the depths of bad behaviour. When the people I loved turned into people I hardly knew, people they themselves could barely recognize. There were nights when I cowered in my room with a pillow over my head to drown out the shouting.

*

Pelting rain bounces knee-high off the pavement. A passing car speeds through a deep puddle and launches a wave of icy water that splashes my legs and trickles down inside my rubber boots. Someone wrapped in a sleeping bag lies on the subway vent in front of Birks jewellery store. Another person huddles in a doorway behind a sheet of cardboard. I wonder what brought them to this. Neglect. Abuse. Poverty. Addiction. Bad decisions. Bad luck. So much misery on this drenched and frigid night.

*

When I was a teenager, my parents' drinking and failing marriage left them distracted and self-absorbed and left me unmoored and untethered, lost and searching. My friend Brian often said of me that I was running, always running. I attended the Woodstock music festival at fifteen. Did drugs and drank. When I was seventeen, I lived for a summer in a hippie commune of Jesus freaks, but religion wasn't an answer. I spent the following summer hitchhiking, often alone, around Alberta and British Columbia. When I was twenty, I lived for a time with my boyfriend in a rusted-out Volkswagen van. In winter, the campground, nestled deep in the rainforest on an island off the coast of British Columbia, was deserted. The sun set early, and nights in the uninsulated van were bone-chillingly damp, dismal, interminable. One December evening, we walked along a dark rural road past a small cottage with a Christmas tree aglow in the window, a sight as welcoming as the beacon of a lighthouse, a searchlight in the wilderness that might find me and rescue me. I imagined the warmth and comfort of the kitchen, the delicious dinner that might be served, the cozy beds piled with down quilts and soft pillows, tantalizingly close yet impossibly out of reach. That night, in the bleak and frigid darkness, huddled in a thin sleeping bag under a musty blanket, I swore to myself that I'd do everything in my power to never again have to camp outside in winter, in the equivalent of a tin can.

*

Throughout my teens and twenties, worry about my parents was a ceaseless undertow that threatened to drag me deep under.

My father, who divorced my mother, went on a ten-year bender and married a non-drinker hoping it would help him stay sober, continued to drink after a doctor warned it would kill him and despite being in and out of hospital, in and out of AA, and in and out of rehab and group homes.

My mother, who lived alone and worked full-time, drank in the evenings and on weekends. She thought her secret was safe until she was called into the boss's office and warned she'd lose her job if things didn't change. Despite everything, Mom provided a strong foundation of support for my sister and me. She wrote and phoned regularly, visited when she could, and helped us financially when we needed it. Her unconditional love, and our close connection, was a precious touchstone in my life, but I worried about her, too.

When my parents finally quit drinking for good it was a momentous event in their lives, and in mine, but by then the decades of constant worry had lodged in my body, left an open wound, slow to heal.

*

I turn and hurry back down Granville Street. The woman's sombre face haunts me. Her pleading voice echoes in my ears. I think of the cold hard looks she's endured. A steady stream of passersby avoiding, ignoring, unseeing, unfeeling. Like me. Oh yes, like me. Shame and regret flush my cheeks as though I've been slapped.

My umbrella bends and bows, battered about by gusty winds and driving rain. The deluge is a grey veil, a watery shroud she's disappeared into. I search up and down the block, check entranceways and alleys. I imagine finding her in the shadows of a gloomy doorway, picture myself pressing a twenty-dollar bill into her palm.

*

One New Year's Eve, when I was in my mid-twenties, I climbed the rickety stairs of a dilapidated warehouse and searched the rave's frenzied dancefloor. I spied a couple across the room kissing passionately, his body pressing against hers, before I realized the man was my former boyfriend, the woman a friend. I clattered back downstairs into the clear mild night and walked all the way to Granville Street. As I neared the Hotel Vancouver, I remembered how soldiers returning from the Second World War found themselves homeless due to a post-war housing crisis. How they "occupied" the empty 1916 hotel, which was slated for demolition, and lived there for years.

I found a cocktail perched on the hotel's window ledge, seemingly untouched, with fresh ice cubes and a slice of lime, and took a small sip. Gin and tonic. I slipped off my high heels and pressed the soles of my stockinged feet onto the cold damp sidewalk. With my shoes in one hand and the cocktail in the other, I wandered home to my apartment in the West End, sipping my drink and wondering whether, it being past midnight, it was too late to make some resolutions.

*

I trudge back up the street, bedraggled and dispirited, past the large Christmas tree on the north plaza of the old Vancouver courthouse, to the Hotel Vancouver.

A few days before, I unpacked a box of Christmas decorations with my long-wished-for late-in-life little family, a gift from the universe I'd once despaired of ever having. I handed the unbreakable ornaments to my three-year-old son to hang up all by himself.

"Thank you, Mama," he said. "For getting these ready for me."

*

Six years after my father's death, Mom died suddenly of a brain aneurysm, a shocking and devastating loss that sent me spiralling off my axis. Not being able to call her was the hardest. For years we talked daily. When the phone rang I still thought it would be her. One morning, I picked up the receiver and dialed before I remembered. I ached to hear her voice, always happy to hear from me. The telephone line. The umbilical cord. Severed forever.

Plagued by restless legs syndrome, a chronic condition I'd suffered from a young age, I couldn't sleep. Night after night, depressed and inconsolable, I drank wine, ate junk food, and watched mindless television as my family slept. My weight ballooned and my eye sockets were sunken and yellow. One morning, in the shower, my fingers filled with long strands of hair, and in the following days more hair fell out. My doctor prescribed antidepressants and sleeping pills, scheduled an appointment with a specialist. The specialist flipped through my test results, and his kind brown eyes met mine.

"I don't know how you get out of bed in the morning," he said.

I was suffering from severe anemia. The doctor had no idea why my iron levels had plummeted so suddenly and drastically, but I knew. The lifeblood had drained from my body. Grief was what was coursing through my veins now.

Months rushed headlong, but time hadn't begun to heal my wounds. Ashamed to admit the magnitude of my mourning, I took my grief underground. Drank alone in the flickering blue light of the television and cried myself to sleep. As the one-year anniversary of Mom's death loomed, I found myself frightened by my fragility, my drinking. Envisioned Mom's concern. Imagined my five-year-old's eyes watching me, unsettled and afraid. *Enough*, I thought. I sat my son down and promised him that although I was very sad, I would be happy again. Some days, I thought, *but never as happy*. Other days, I thought, *at least happier than this?*

As the saying goes, you must keep living until you're alive again. Each morning I tried to think of something, anything, to make me feel better. The one thing was swimming. The healing embrace of water, the fluid motion, comfortingly familiar.

My son fell in love with a Peter Rabbit video, which he watched again and again. In the video, Peter's mother warns him not to go into Mr. McGregor's garden, but Peter cannot resist the rows of lettuce and beans and radishes, and despite the danger, sneaks in. When Mr. McGregor spots him, Peter runs for his life, losing first one shoe and then the other, until he trips and falls, and the brass buttons on his jacket get caught in a gooseberry net. Peter struggles to free himself, and he begins to lose heart. Some friendly sparrows hear his sobs and implore him to continue.

"Don't give up!" they cry. "Never give up!"

I joined Weight Watchers, drank less, and swam and swam and swam. Many more months passed, and on those days when I felt sad and missed Mom, when my buttons got stuck in a gooseberry bush, I remembered Peter Rabbit and imagined friendly sparrows circling me, urging me on. And on I went.

*

The lobby of the Hotel Vancouver is decorated with glittering Christmas trees and twinkling white lights and festive garlands. I find the oak-panelled room where the party is in full swing and duck into the ladies' washroom. I hang up my sopping wet coat, open my umbrella to dry, swap my rubber boots for heels, smooth the damp creases in my best dress, and fix my hair and makeup in the ornate mirror. As I apply a fresh coat of lipstick, my gaze shifts to my eyes. Did I imagine the woman on the street to be a witch in a fairy tale? Able to conjure a swap and turn me into her? Drag me back to a time and a place I left behind? How often I've felt on the outside looking in. How close I've come, over the years, to falling between the cracks and into dark places. It seems I've always existed in a liminal space, in a nether land between my past and present, between who I might have been and who I ended up becoming.

*

How could I have predicted that a decade after that dark rain-drenched night, as I rinsed empty wine bottles after a dinner party, my twelve-year-old son would remark—did you guys drink all that? That, soon after, I'd quit drinking for good. That many years later my adult son would mention a guy he knows who's a recovering addict. That the conversation would prompt me to cautiously ask which drugs he's tried. That he would pause for a moment, as if searching for the right words, as I braced myself for his answer.

"I haven't tried anything," he said finally.

"Nothing?"

"Nothing. I thought I might like it too much, you know?"

*

I imagine the woman, that night, the rain. She stops running. Surrenders to the deluge. Raises her face to the sky as raindrops and tears flow together down her cheeks. Suddenly a warm raincoat wraps around her body and boots protect her feet. She stands straight and tall, and opens her umbrella. A sheet of rain streams from it, forming a perfect circle, a liquid force field, around her.

# Contributors

**Kate Bird**'s creative nonfiction has been published in *Queen's Quarterly*, *The Sun*, *Prairie Fire*, *The Humber Literary Review*, and other literary journals. She won third prize in the 2022 Prairie Fire MRB Creative Non-Fiction Contest, her work was longlisted for the CBC Nonfiction Prize and the Edna Staebler Personal Essay Contest, and she was featured on *Writers Radio*. Kate is a graduate of The Writer's Studio at Simon Fraser University and the Vancouver Manuscript Intensive. She is the author of three books of newspaper photography, including the bestselling *Vancouver in the Seventies: Photos from A Decade That Changed the City*, which was nominated for the 2016 British Columbia Historical Writing Award, and has been the researcher for numerous books, including *Making Headlines: 100 Years of The Vancouver Sun*, which won the Bill Duthie Booksellers' Choice Award at the 2013 BC Book Prizes. Kate recently received a Professional Development grant from Access Copyright to work on a collection of personal essays. You can find Kate at katebird.ca

**Tove Black** has an MFA from the University of British Columbia and lives in East Vancouver, on the unceded lands of the xʷməθkʷəy'əm (Musqueam), Sḵwx̱wú7mesh (Squamish), and səl̓ilw̓ətaʔɬ (Tsleil-Waututh) Nations. She writes and illustrates literary zines, her novella *Lonesome Stars* placed third in the 2022 3-Day Novel Contest, and you can hear one of her recent stories at *The Tahoma Literary Review*'s Soundcloud.

**James Boutin-Crawford** - Loving husband, devoted father and grandfather, true friend.

**Jessica Cole** is an artist and writer based in Vancouver, originally hailing from Calgary. With a lifelong passion for storytelling in all its forms, she delights in blurring the lines between reality and fiction. Whether through visual mediums or the written word, Jessica invites readers into her world, crafting stories that feel like pages from a personal diary stumbled upon by chance. Her work captures the dreamy, poetic essence of everyday life. *Off the Map* marks Jessica's second official publication, following her first experience in print at the age of nine, when her short story was featured in a young writer's anthology series. Currently, she works as a freelance art director and photographer for fashion brands, and in her spare time, she enjoys writing, visiting local cafés, and playing *Slime Rancher*.

**Crisi Corby** is a mother, an activist, and a personal essay writer living on the unceded traditional territories of the xʷməθkʷəy'əm (Musqueam), Sk̲wx̲wú7mesh (Squamish), and səl̓ilw̓ətaʔɬ (Tsleil-Waututh) Nations. Her storytelling is influenced by her East Van upbringing, and the intricacies of navigating motherhood through societal pressure and mental health issues. Crisi uses writing as a way to raise awareness for social and political issues, and to spark meaningful conversations.

**Gilles Cyrenne** has self-published a book of poetry, *Emerge*, and, with help from Vancouver Manuscript Intensive, has assembled a book of poetry and short memoir that is ready to go to press. He grew up as a farmer/cowboy in Southwest Saskatchewan but now thrives as an urban monkey in the creative chaos of Vancouver's Downtown Eastside. He regularly publishes political rants and poetry in the *Carnegie Newsletter*, served for five years as President of the Carnegie Community Centre Association, and is now the Board's Vice President. He coordinates the DTES Writers Collective and leads a writing group at the Gathering Place Community Centre and an ESL Conversation class. He is a founding member and organizer of the DTES Writers Festival, now in planning for its fourth iteration. Cyrenne is a member of the Megaphone Shift Peer Group. He publishes monthly in *Megaphone*, a street magazine, and his articles have been picked up by local newspapers across Canada. He was long-listed in Pulp Fiction's Kingfisher short poem contest, and is published in *From the Heart of it All: Ten Years of Writing from Vancouver's Downtown Eastside*, as well as several anthologies from Thursdays Writing Collective. He has also won the poetry and essay writing contests in the Carnegie Newsletter's Sandy Cameron Memorial Writing contest and the Best DTES poem in the Muriel's Journey Poetry Prize contest. When not reading and writing, he continues to build stuff with wood for fun, a continuation of a carpentry career that helped him survive and recover from his addiction to alcohol.

**Venge Dixon** is a white settler writer, poet, visual artist, comic book creator, and musician. She's a nonbinary lesbian who has lived with mental illness all her life. Her creative work is a deliberate (and occasionally accidental) reflection of this experience. Venge chose creative work to step outside the many externally assigned, designed, and forcefully imposed boxes she saw as surrounding each of us and most punishingly, those of us who experience our lives outside of societal norms or within marginalized communities. Creating became a means not only of self-definition but of personal responsibility in a confusing world which defines her and many others as Crazy.

**Jaki Eisman** is a graduate of The Writer's Studio at SFU, and her work can be found in *Emerge 21*, *Room*, *Open Minds Quarterly*, and the recent anthology *Better Next Year*. She is currently writing a tragicomic memoir about the challenges, victories, and spiritual opportunities of a life spent dealing with mental illness. She lives in Vancouver with her fluffy cat, Nunu.

**Christy Frisken** is a multi-disciplinary artist and writer residing in the city of Vancouver, where the Fraser River meets the Salish Sea, on the unceded lands of the xʷməθkʷəy'əm (Musqueam), Sḵwx̱wú7mesh (Squamish), and səl̓ilw̓ətaʔɬ (Tsleil-Waututh) Nations. She is the fourth daughter of a Scottish-born father and a mother of English and Scottish settler descent. After working for over 15 years as a bicycle messenger, Christy graduated from Emily Carr University of Art + Design in 2012 with a major in Visual Arts. Her artwork has been exhibited in various galleries such as Access Gallery, Richmond Art Gallery, and Surrey Art Gallery. "A Faulty Compass" is her first creative nonfiction essay to be published in print.

**Merle Ginsburg** moved from Ottawa to Vancouver a lifetime ago. She's been writing non-fiction and poetry off and on for many years. She recently made the decision to take herself seriously as a writer. She created a column entitled "Musings from Lived Experience" for people with lived/living experience of mental health and/or substance use issues. She writes about her colourful childhood and the people, places, and things she sees in the world around her. She is curious, detail oriented, compassionate, and knows how fortunate she is to have a good sense of humour. She is immensely grateful for the gift of writing.

**Angela J. Gray** (she/her) is an emerging Black writer and visual artist living in Vancouver, BC. She practices on the stolen lands of the xʷməθkʷəy̓əm (Musqueam), Sḵwx̱wú7mesh (Squamish), and səl̓ilw̓ətaʔɬ (Tsleil-Waututh) Nations. Angela writes about the impact of colonization on children of the African/Caribbean Diaspora who have been adopted into white homes. Her work has appeared in *Periodicities: a journal of poetry and poetics*, the Red Cross National Bulletin - Black History Month, and *The Capilano Review* "From the Archives" newsletter. She is a Canada Council for the Arts grant recipient. Angela has also spoken on the *Medicine for the Resistance* podcast and has been a part of the Massy Arts Society–Voices Series. Angela is a graduate of Vancouver Manuscript Intensive, and a Creative and Culture Consultant/Facilitator. She is currently seeking a publisher for her memoir *A Clean House*.

**Adishi Gupta** (she/her) moved to Vancouver in 2021 to pursue her graduate studies at the University of British Columbia. She holds an advanced certification in *Writing Lives* from the University of Oxford. Her writing journey, spanning over a decade, includes creative nonfiction, poetry, and opinion pieces published in *Feminism in India*, *Mad in Asia Pacific*, and *The Swaddle*. Her writing has also appeared in three anthologies: *The Side Effects of Living*, *DU Love*, and *After Dickens*. She sporadically writes a Substack newsletter titled *Tender Tales*. She deeply loves life writing because of its magical power to make people feel seen and heard. When she's not working, you will likely find her sky gazing or dreaming up her next collage.

**Jean Kavanagh** began her writing life as a reporter and for many years has worked in communications. She doesn't consider herself a "real" writer, but tries now and again. Programs like Simon Fraser University's The Writer's Studio have helped.

**Yong Nan Kim** was born in Busan, Korea, and lived in Paraguay and Brazil in the 1970s and 80s. She then immigrated to the US and studied Spanish language & literature at the University of Virginia and Universidad de Valencia in Spain. She also holds a master's degree in Iberian and Latin American Linguistics from the University of Texas. In 2001, she moved to Vancouver, BC, where she currently resides, and has worked as an interpreter, translator, and sessional lecturer at UBC and SFU. During her time in The Writer's Studio at Simon Fraser University in 2019, she studied poetry and wrote *My Year Without Books*, a memoir about her childhood and adolescence in Paraguay and Brazil. An excerpt was published in the *Emerge 19 TWS Anthology*. The selected poems in *Off the Map* are excerpts from her current work in progress, a speculative memoir about her family's silent history during the Russian and Japanese occupation of Korea and the Korean War. It examines intergenerational trauma as well as the author's own experiences of mental illness. By weaving in dreams, memories of ancestors, ghost stories, and Korean folktales, Yong confronts a complex history and heritage by writing into their silence.

**Justyna Krol** is a writer and graphic designer from Lublin, Poland, now living on the traditional and unceded territories of the xʷməθkʷəy'əm (Musqueam), Sḵwx̱wú7mesh (Squamish), and səl̓ilw̓ətaʔɬ (Tsleil-Waututh) Nations, also known as Vancouver, BC. She spends her time writing, designing, and talking to crows. She hates mornings, loves sugar, and uses the latter to get through the former.

**jerry LaFaery** is a Generalist, playing and surviving in a variety of mediums including this one. Practising live-performance, within community and commercial work spaces. Living as a 'Q' member of the rainbow, and occupying space somewhere on the spectrum of fantasy to reality™, appearing frequently on a land contestably referred to as Vancouver, Canada. From their POV, if the world has to be divided into two groups, then 'Diagnosed and Undiagnosed' might be a fun place to start.

**Danica Longair** (she/her) is a disabled mom and writer trying to crawl out from under her two young boys, tuxedo cat, and lifelong depression to get her hands to her keyboard. She is a graduate/survivor of SFU's The Writer's Studio, 2020—The Pandemic Cohort. Her writing has appeared in *Prairie Fire* and *The New Quarterly*, the anthologies *Sustenance* and *The Walls Between Us*, and has been a finalist for contests with CANSCAIP, *Room*, *PRISM International*, and *The Fiddlehead*. She is currently working on a novel about stigma: imagining the eventual dystopian outcome of scapegoating the mentally ill for violence. Find out more about her at www.danicalongair.com.

**Harry McKeown**'s debut chapbook *i need not be good* was published in February 2022 by Rahila's Ghost Press and shortlisted for the 2023 bpNichol Chapbook Award. Their poems are forthcoming or have appeared in *SAD Mag*, *Poetry Magazine*, *Room*, *Peach Mag*, *Poetry is Dead*, *The Ex-Puritan*, and *Bad Nudes*. They were awarded the George McWhirter Prize for Poetry in Winter 2020.

**Neven Marelj** is a poet, care and events worker. Their multi-genre work has appeared in places such as *Room*, Hatch Gallery, James Black Gallery, and *Of Our Own Making* (League of Canadian Poets 2024). They are the 2024 recipient of the George McWhirter Prize in Poetry. They think a lot about archives.

Based in East Vancouver, BC, **Quin Martins** is a multidisciplinary artist and writer who draws inspiration from his journey with mental health and substance use. Through humour, Quin likes to explore themes common to speculative fiction, such as questions of authorship in the digital age and the delicate balance between personal creativity and corporate influence. He holds a BFA in visual arts from the Emily Carr University of Art and Design. His non-fiction writing has appeared in *SAD Mag*.

**Pari Mokradi** (he/they) is a multidisciplinary artist and writer whose practice is deeply rooted in their lived experience as a South Asian settler on the unceded lands of Vancouver's Downtown Eastside. A self-taught creator, Pari engages with the local community to explore themes of memory and mythology. Their recent accolades include the Sandy Cameron Memorial Award at the DTES Heart of the City

Festival, First Prize in Visual Art from the Surrey Art Gallery, and the prestigious Aruna D'Souza Award from the Southern Alberta Art Gallery. Their chapbook, *DTES Watching*, is forthcoming with Pinhole Poetry in Summer 2025. Connect with Pari on Instagram at @pari.mokradi or explore their work at www.paricreative.com

**Ronan Nanning-Watson** (he/they) is an interdisciplinary artist, writer, and educator who lives and works on unceded Coast Salish territory, AKA Vancouver, BC. They create imaginative portals to connect viewers to other worlds and dimensions that they have experienced through brain injuries and neurodivergence. Their work is grounded in the practical constraints of living with a disability in a rigged/brutal/beautiful world but always reaches for the sublime and transcendent. Their work connects and mutates across many genres and is always inseparable from self-accommodation, community building, learning, and healing.

**Rye Orrange** is a trans writer born and raised in "Vancouver, BC." He has been using writing as a creative outlet and self-preservation tool since his childhood years. Rye's work has been included in a variety of zines, anthologies, and digital magazines, often exploring topics of gender, mental health, and addiction. Rye hopes to one day live in a world free of stigma and criminalization for people who use substances, by any means possible.

**Mary Phyllis O'Toole** - I have a theory that when a group of people, whether Afro-American, LGBTQ, mentally ill people, etc., are oppressed, their way up is through asserting themselves through their culture, whether art, literature, or music. This is one of the reasons I write, not only for emotional catharsis, but to shine a light on schizophrenia.

**Bruce Ray** - My journey has been a long one. I was diagnosed with schizophrenia when I was twenty one years old—now I am sixty. I am an artist and a poet. I have been a part of the collective Gallery Gachet for two decades. It is a community of those who have mental illness and also practice art. I have put on five solo shows and participated in various group events. I have self-published two chapbooks of poetry and a graphic novel. I had a book of cartoon stories published by Boxer Press in 2018 called *I Threw a Brick through a Window*. I think of myself as a survivor and not a victim. In disability there is hidden ability and in difficulty there is opportunity. I have lived through trauma and come to the other side. I believe that art and politics are linked in the expression and act of creation. I believe that we must struggle for justice and share stories—all those who bear the stigma of mental illness. As I educate myself on the business of art and I educate the public, it's all a part of the process. I think that optimism and positivity are both necessities for our lives. To change with the times we must adapt. In this way, the outsider (as they call us) must be reunited with the community. We must offer our talents and contribute to society. In conclusion I would say that the only solution is empowerment and self-direction. I am not defined by my disease. This is the way I am because this is the way I was made.

**Ingrid Rose** - My writing has appeared most recently in *Don't Tell: Family Secrets*, edited by Donna Sharkey and Arleen Paré, 2023. I've been teaching "writing from the body" online since 2019. I'm co-producer and co-host of writersradio.ca now in its 5th year. My memoir, *re/membering :: essays & other stories* will be out this fall, 2025.

**Beth Rowntree** lives in Vancouver. She is neurodiverse, and imprecisely diagnosed as living with schizophrenia and autism, or possibly with some other yet to be defined disorder. A psychiatrist once said her brain had "shrunk." Perhaps her brain is down to its essence. Her writing has been published in *Hidden Lives: true stories from people who live with mental illness*, *Geist Magazine*, *Exile Quarterly*, *Fig:ment Magazine*, and *The Best of the Best Canadian Poetry in English*.

**Lenore Rowntree** lives in Vancouver. Her linked collection of stories *See You Later Maybe Never* (NON Press, 2022) is a humorous exploration of the dilemmas of aging. Her novel *Cluck* (Thistledown Press, 2016) is about Henry, an only child growing up with a mother who lives with bipolar disorder. Lenore is the lead editor and contributor to *Hidden Lives: true stories from people who live with mental illness* (Touchwood Editions, 2nd ed. 2017). Her poetry, short stories, and essays have been published in several anthologies, magazines, and newspapers, including *Geist Magazine*, *Exile Quarterly*, *The New Quarterly*, *The Best of the Best Canadian Poetry in English*, and *The Globe & Mail*.

**Kim Seary** is a Jessie Award–winning actress. As a writer/performer, she presented *Madame Scotch-tape* at the Montreal Fringe and at Women in View in Vancouver, and *The Beautiful Thing*, an original musical, for the Kickstart Festival. Other plays include *Hot Flashes—on the Rocky Road to Redemption* with Christine Willes at the Telus Stage of the Chan Centre, and *Magdalena's Monster* for Origins Theatre Projects at Pacific Theatre. Kim's stories include "Patricia" in *My Mother's Story* anthology, and "I do" in the anthology *Concussion: Not Just Another Head-line*. Her poem "Window of Slow" was published in *Quills Canadian Poetry Magazine*. With Pandora's Poetry Collective, Kim has read for events such as Twisted Poets and Poetic Pairings. She has also read her work at SFU's The Writer's Studio Reading Series. Kim has studied with teachers such as Heather Conn, Betsy Warland, Bonnie Nish, and Shauna Paull, and has hosted numerous writing circles. She was producer of *The Bodacious Reading Series for Women Playwrights* at Presentation House Theatre. Her poetry manuscript *Beyond the Veil* (working title), is currently in progress. Kim is a member of the Federation of BC Writers.

**Seema Shah** is a self-taught visual artist and writer living in Vancouver, BC, unceded Coast Salish Territory. Working mainly in the medium of collage, she frequently incorporates text into her artwork. Her creative nonfiction has been published in literary journals and anthologies, shortlisted for the Canadian Lesbian & Gay Archives' Narrative Essay Contest and twice for the Surrey International Writers' Conference Contest, and longlisted for the Susan Crean Award for Nonfiction 2023. Her artwork has been exhibited in galleries in Canada, the US, and the UK, and appeared in publications including *SAD Magazine* and *Contemporary Collage Magazine*. Seema was a recipient of The Beaumont Studios' Artist To Watch Award 2022 and a highly commended artist in the 2022 & 2023 Contemporary Collage Magazine Awards. seemashahart.com

**Neko Smart** lives on xʷməθkʷəy'əm land. They are a graduate of UBC's BFA Creative Writing program. As 2020 Victoria City Youth Poet Laureate, they emphasised the importance of cultivating open dialogue about mental health in order to reduce stigma and increase safety. They're a member of the Wordplay poetry workshop facilitation roster and the former slam coordinator for the UBC Slam Poetry Club. They were a finalist in the 2023 and 2024 Canadian Individual Poetry Slams.

**Amy Wang** is a Chinese-Canadian writer born and raised in Vancouver, BC. Their work has been published in *Paper Shell*, *That's What [We] Said*, *The Goose*, and *The Garden Statuary,* and exhibited in IGNITE! Youth-Driven Arts Festival. They are currently an MFA student at the University of British Columbia (Okanagan).

**Sandra Yuen** is an artist, writer, and public speaker on recovery. After earning a Fine Arts Diploma from Langara College and a Bachelor of Arts from the University of British Columbia in art history, she received the Courage to Come Back Award and the Queen Elizabeth II Diamond Jubilee Medal. Under the pen name Sandra Yuen MacKay, she published *My Schizophrenic Life: The Road to Recovery from Mental Illness* (Bridgeross Communications, 2010), *Chop Shtick* (2016), and *From New York to Vancouver: Stories on the Fly* co-written with James D. Young (2018). She has published numerous mental health articles for magazines. Also she has a poetry book in the works titled *I Want to Be Buried Standing Up*. As an artist, she paints florals, house portraits, and abstracts using acrylics and oils. She enjoys playing drums for Beautiful Lizards. She has lived experience of mental illness, residing in Vancouver BC.

# Editors

**Betsy Warland** is the author of fourteen books of creative nonfiction, memoir, and poetry, and has been a manuscript consultant and editor for more than 30 years. Betsy is an established figure in the Canadian literary community and is deeply committed to community and collaboration. Throughout her career, she has been dedicated to emerging writers. In 2011, She received Pandora's Literary Festival BC Writer Mentor Award. Betsy founded and was the previous Director of The Writers Studio at SFU and the Vancouver Manuscript Intensive, and continues to teach in both programs. She received the City of Vancouver Mayor's Award for Literary Excellence in 2016. In 2022, an annual national prize, The VMI Betsy Warland Between Genres Award, was launched. Betsy has significant experience editing collections of writing, including literary anthologies (e.g., InVersions: Writing by Dykes, Queers, and Lesbians) and special issues of literary journals (e.g., The Malahat Review - Queer Perspectives Issue guest editor).

**Seema Shah** is a self-taught visual artist and writer with lived experience of mental health issues who resides in Vancouver, BC, unceded Coast Salish Territory. Her creative nonfiction has been published in literary journals and anthologies, shortlisted for the Canadian Lesbian & Gay Archives' Narrative Essay Contest and twice for the Surrey International Writers' Conference Contest, and longlisted for the Susan Crean Award for Nonfiction 2023. Her artwork has been exhibited in galleries in Canada, the US, and the UK, and she was a recipient of The Beaumont Studios' Artist To Watch Award 2022. Alongside her own creative practice, Seema is the organizer of Professional Artistic Growth Made Accessible, a project that offers free professional development opportunities to Vancouver artists and writers with lived experience of mental health and/or substance use issues, including workshops and consultations. This project laid the groundwork for *Off the Map*. As part of the project, Seema has co-curated four gallery exhibitions with Yuri Arajs, Director and Curator at Outsiders and Others in Vancouver. seemashahart.com

**Kate Bird**'s creative nonfiction has been published in *Queen's Quarterly*, *The Sun*, *Prairie Fire*, *The Humber Literary Review*, and other literary journals, and she recently received a Professional Development grant from Access Copyright to work on a collection of personal essays. A professional librarian with a master's degree in Library and Information Science, Kate has been the researcher for numerous books, including *Making Headlines: 100 Years of The Vancouver Sun*, which won the Bill Duthie Booksellers' Choice Award at the 2013 BC Book Prizes, and *Lilies and Fireweed: Frontier Women of British Columbia*. She is the author of three books of newspaper photography, including the bestselling *Vancouver in the Seventies: Photos from A Decade That Changed the City*, which was nominated for the 2016 British Columbia Historical Writing Award, as well as *City On Edge: A Rebellious Century of Vancouver Protests, Riots and Strikes* and *Magic Moments in BC Sports: A Century in Photos*. You can find Kate at katebird.ca

www.ingramcontent.com/pod-product-compliance
Lightning Source LLC
Jackson TN
JSHW010011220425
83009JS00007B/20
* 9 7 8 1 7 3 8 7 1 6 7 8 4 *